Who You Callin' SILLY?

How a Silly Woman Becomes Virtuous

KIMBERLY R. LOCK

Copyright ©2012 by Kimberly R. Lock. All rights reserved.

Limit of Liability/Disclaimer of Warranty: While the publisher and author have used their best efforts in preparing this book, they make no representations or warranties with respect to the accuracy or completeness of the contents of this book and specifically disclaim any implied warranties of merchantability or fitness for a particular purpose.

Library of Congress Cataloging-in-Publication Data

LCCN: 2017905585

Who You Callin' Silly? How a Silly Woman Becomes Virtuous
Lock, Kimberly R.

ISBN: 978-0-9987208-2-1
10 9 8 7 6 5 4 3 2 1
Printed and Bound in the United States of America

A Publication of KRL Publishing

EVERYTHING WE TOUCH TURNS TO GOLD

krlpublishing@gmail.com

Who can find
a virtuous
woman?

For her price is
far above rubies.

—Proverbs 31:10

Dedication

This book is dedicated to first, my Lord and Savior Jesus Christ. I only took the words that have been written before time through the Bible, and applied them to real-life scenarios women face today. I don't live, breathe or think without you; the vision was planted because of you and I will never take credit. All glory and honor belongs to you and I thank you for allowing me to do this in your name.

To my husband, Marlon, who is my inspiration and visionary. It was through you allowing the Lord to use you, as always, that I received confirmation to proceed with this effort and realized truly what the Lord's will is for my life; because of your total surrender, dedication, and commitment to the Lord, He brought us together. I sincerely love you with a love that's indescribable by any words that I can place on paper.

To my four daughters, Toney, India, Asia, Sydney and my son Marlon Jr. Before I married your dad, I couldn't imagine having this many children in my life and now I can't imagine life without you! This book is proof that you can do whatever you desire, as long as it aligns with the will of God. Please remember who you are and to keep the Lord first and remember mommy will always be there for you.

This book is also dedicated to my mothers for your love and support in any and every way.

Finally, this book is dedicated to the women from all walks of life, who refuse to walk through life being defined by stereotypes, stigmas and self-centered individuals. This book is a small portion of our journey to being virtuous!

Contents

Foreword vii

Introduction xi

Part One: All My Single Ladies

Chapter 1 Who You Callin' Silly? 1

Chapter 2 The Realization 3

Chapter 3 The Commitment 15
How Clean is Your Temple?

Chapter 4 Love 33

Chapter 5 So Just What is a Silly Woman? 41
The Daughter of Herodias
Delilah
I was Silly, Too!

Part Two: "I's Married Na!"

Chapter 6 Vows 55
For Better or for Worse
For Richer or Poorer
In Sickness and In Health

Chapter 7	How to Be a Wife *Guide the House*	71
Chapter 8	Parenting *How Do You Train a Child?*	75
Chapter 9	Discretion	81
Chapter 10	Love, as God Loves	89
Chapter 11	The Sacrifice	95
Chapter 12	Can I Be a Silly Wife? *Sapphira* *Bathsheba* *Job's Wife* *Eve*	103

Part Three: Every Woman

Chapter 13	Forgiveness	115
Chapter 14	Potentially Silly Questions and the Virtuous Answers	119

Conclusion	136
Epilogue	139
About the Author	143
Acknowledgments	145
Notes	148

Foreword

Reading this phenomenal book is *you! Who You Callin' Silly* will not only transform your life, but restore you spiritually. Allow your transformation to develop a deeper relationship with God as Author Kimberly Lock shares her testimony, revelations and spiritual knowledge that God has given her to write this book in an effort to spiritually help "all" women.

The biblical truths author Kimberly Lock shares throughout the chapters will spiritually examine and address issues for women who are married or single. The message is crystal clear: it is important for you to consider what the word of God says for your life and to be determined to look with new spiritual eyes beyond your past.

In Proverbs 31:10, "Who can find a virtuous woman? for her price is far above rubies," the scripture indicates that this woman is a rare treasure and priceless to God. Possessing Godly characteristics is not optional, but essential.

One day I asked God how He saw my character. He told me to look in His spiritual mirror, the Bible, James 1:22-25(KJV). The word of God showed me a reflection of my character "flaws." With a ministry calling on my life, I had been living in bondage. I had to take ownership of my sins and confess to God. Taking ownership of your sins is a mandatory step in the process of being delivered and healed. After my cry and confession, God stripped down my walls of sin, then rebuilt and transformed my heart and character with His Spirit. Apostle Elbridge Lock, the founder of Unity Gospel House of Prayer in Milwaukee, Wisconsin, ordained me as an Evangelist to preach and teach the Gospel of Jesus Christ. His grandson, Pastor Marlon Lock, ordained me to be an Eldress to assist and help develop the body of Christ.

In my ministry, I have labored with and counseled hundreds of women with broken spirits, i.e., preachers, house-wives, pastor wives, students, educators, single women, women with suicide spirits, and women in shelters, mental health institutions, and prisons. God has given me the spiritual authority to minister to women.

Kimberly Lock has the character and reputation of a holy woman, which was developed through a process of sacrifice, dedication and submission, and through many trials and temptations. Therefore, ladies, do the assessments she offers in her book to examine, your faults, fruit and character.

Women, if you have been rejected because you have fallen short of the expectations of others, know that God's word destroys the root of rejection! You will see that this book is a voice for the voiceless as you read the testimony of Kim Lock, who kept her testimony voiceless inside her for years. Many women are voiceless, because they have been abused and beaten down by life circumstances and have been told they have no purpose. As a result, they feel they have nothing to contribute. Allow this anointed book to be a ministering tool to deliver and set you free from shame, unforgiveness, resentment, stored-up anger, regrets, emotional damage, low self-esteem, ungodly relationships, sexual abuse, sexual temptation and having a manipulative spirit.

To women in ministry, many say "I know God," when

they only know of Him, because they don't live the lifestyle of holiness and purification. Therefore, your ministry has been stagnated, meaning sluggish, dull and not flowing. Women in ministry, as you read this book allow God's Spirit to challenge you to align your character with His Holy character and watch God elevate your ministry.

Who You Callin' Silly challenges you to look into the spiritual mirror, the Bible, to see your character and spirit. Pray before you read, and develop questions to ask God to answer regarding your life. For example, does your character line up with God's character? Do you have a meek spirit? Are you an adaptable woman, willing to submit and allow God to change you? Are you a woman of faith? Are you saved? Let God's Spirit cleanse and develop you to reflect His image as you embrace reading this Holy Spirit-filled book.

The devil will make you a silly proposition just like he made Eve in the Garden of Eden. Don't eat his fruit! Who you callin' silly? Ladies, let's take our journey to develop deeper spiritually!

— Eldress, Rhonda Cotton

Introduction

I have a story to share, a testimony inside of me that has lain dormant. I have not always desired to share my story as I would consider myself reserved; however, the desire was so overwhelming that I had to begin this process.

Oftentimes, we have certain places we go where we can have an intimate moment with God. Other times, it happens anywhere. There is no set or appointed time to worship the Lord or hear Him speak to us. For me, my time often comes when I'm going to the salon. Not only do I look forward to my hair looking good, I'm also excited to see what the Lord will share with me. However, this particular time was different than the others. Sometimes, the Lord would give me a scripture and the understanding of it while at the hair salon; however, this time, it began in bed, the night before my hair appointment. Whenever I would go to the hair salon and He would give me a word, I would then go home and send what He gave me to the women at church, to whom I had already sent daily devotions via email. Sending daily devotional emails came about earlier when I was a Systems Analyst/Project Manager.

Think about this: when we arrive to work in the morning, we grab our coffee or breakfast and dive right in to our workday. There's no acknowledgement or thank you to the Lord for another day, nor a request for His blessing that the day is productive, nor a prayer that an issue we've been dealing with at work is resolved. Receiving daily devotions for myself made me take a deep breath, honor and recognize Jesus FIRST, and then start my day. I thought others could benefit as well and so I began sending them to a few co-workers and sisters from church. I'd then receive requests from people who had received a forwarded copy of the devotion, to include them on the recipient list. Fast-forwarding to the revelation….this time, the Lord had given me a word about women…single ladies in particular, which then expanded to married women as well. I quickly ran to the gas station before my appointment and purchased a writing tablet, so I could jot down notes while seated under the dryer. After my stylist had worked his magic on my hair, I went home that afternoon, sat at my laptop, Bible and tablet nearby, and began typing.

The response I received from recipients of the seven-page email was overwhelming. The email would be sent to over 150 women from the church, family and friends. Responses flew in as the recipients of the email forwarded it on to co-workers and their family members, some even asking if they could take the material and use it at their church's single ladies class. I couldn't take credit for that material and I certainly wouldn't dare. I thank God that it touched someone's life as it did mine and that they were able to see themselves or forward on to help someone else.

I wasn't shocked at how the Lord was able to use me because I had made myself a vessel for his use fourteen years ago; but I was more shocked of how well it was written. You see, this was coming from someone who absolutely **ABHORRED** writing and English 101 in College. English was never my choice subject, nor communications. I couldn't understand why I had to take a class for a language that I already knew how to speak. It's not like I was trying to learn Spanish or French; it's English, people!!! I had been speaking it for over sixteen years. To sit in a class and learn pronunciation, grammatical errors and uses of terminology…I had no pleasure in it. On the other hand, I was completely drawn to technology, math and science, which led to the Lord allowing me to obtain a Bachelor's degree in Management Information Systems and a Master's Degree in Telecommunications.

The word quickly spread and the Pastor of my church, who also happens to be my husband, caught wind of it. He even stated during a sermon that I should start a class for single ladies. For anyone who knows me, I consult the Lord about everything…cooking, direction to travel when leaving the house, how to spend my money, what to read in His word…***EVERYTHING!*** Although my husband is a powerful man of God, I expressed to him (which he was fully aware) that I cannot teach a class unless the Lord says. The Lord had not spoken to me to be a minister or a teacher at our church. To take on an obligation such as teaching a ladies class, being responsible for EVERY word spoken to these women…honey, Jesus HIMSELF would have to speak. Why shouldn't I desire that? If He spoke to my husband at age five to preach His word, well…He's the same, right? Jesus said He would never change and He's the same today, yesterday and forever (Hebrews 13:8). Surely if He spoke to my husband thirty-plus years ago, He could speak to me now! Not to mention, we already had a spiritual guidance class for all women, regardless of age or marital status; but this class would have been single ladies only. So…I did not start a class.

Five months had passed and it was a September afternoon of Thursday Evening Bible Class. I had just sent an email to a young lady at church who had asked if I could send her words of encouragement and prayer for some storms in her life that she had been dealing with. I shared with my husband what I had sent to her. He responded by saying that the email was powerful and if I only knew what gift the Lord had given me through writing. Gift? As me and my husband would say, Chileplease which means "child please" (a statement that my husband and I would make often about an unbelievable situation)! Remember this is someone (me) who doesn't jump at the opportunity to write. The only thing I know how to do when someone is seeking advice, desires words of encouragement or cries for help is to first acknowledge God and ask Him to give me what to say. You see, my words and your words are opinionated, debatable and arguable; but one thing we cannot do is argue against the Word of God. His words have stood the test of time and He means JUST what He says.

That September Thursday evening Bible study, the Pastor called on who He calls "the panel." These are ministers that the Pastor selects to assist him in teaching on specific topics that the Pastor determines. These four ministers, in addition to the Pastor, expound on the topic through the Word of God, with the Pastor acting as narrator. This is to give the congregation an array of perspectives on the Word of God, so that it is relatable and understandable. One of the ladies on the panel read a scripture that confirmed the burning in my heart to proceed with writing this book. And so, the journey begins here! Me... and you...together.

I invite you to take this self-examination journey with me and experience a narrative so powerful through the Spirit of God that you will forever change the way you view yourself as a woman. Allow yourself to let down your guard and think about what's about to be imparted into your life. I am by no means an expert in women's study or marriage counseling by man's definition and you may even wonder as I did...what's my credibility? Yes, I had started writing and became discouraged and I even ask the Lord how is it that I am credible in this subject? I studied technology. I'm not a minister or a teacher of the word of God. I don't have any women's organizations that I have founded. I enjoy doing what God has placed upon me to do, which is raise and nurture children unto Him (who will grow up to be God-fearing and admonish HIM), assist my husband on the business aspects of having a congregation and implementing technical solutions within the church. So once again, what's my credibility? Who made me credible? Jesus made me credible, so there you have it! Without Him, none of this would be possible.

During this process I read no other books or periodicals, just the Bible (King James Version) because I wanted to solely depend on Jesus for his guidance, persuasion and inspiration. You will find throughout this book, I reference the Word of God and I provide the actual scripture. Why? He is the foundation. He is the author and chief editor of this book. In addition, there may be someone reading this book that does not have a Bible or does not know how to search the scriptures and understand what they mean. It's the Word of God that changes us. You see, before giving my life to Christ, I was heading nowhere fast and didn't even know it. My thinking was: since I had my education, I would be fine and doing well…I HAD MADE IT! However, I soon learned that what I was doing with my life outside of my career was not working for me and only hindered me. When I TOTALLY submitted my life to the Lord, HE changed me. For that, I am forever indebted to Him.

If this book can touch one life…one woman…to have a more positive outlook on life and understand her worth, then writing it was not in vain. If you as a reader are a non-believer, you will still be able to obtain valuable information to apply to your life. Take the information that you'll obtain to strengthen your inner being that much more or to help someone else in need. If you are as I was and you've realized that what you're doing is not working, give Jesus a try; what do you have to lose? Imagine being a parent or if you have no children, imagine your parents creating a life journal for you that gives you instruction on how to face every obstacle, every challenge, every fear and every event you will encounter in your life, to make your life rewarding. If you follow this journal, you will receive an inheritance they have set aside just for you. That's what God has done. HE is our father; He gave us a life journal (The Bible) and with every situation we face in life, there is an instance in the Bible of how that situation or event was handled according to God's word and according to the fleshy desires of man. And if we choose to follow the Word of God exactly as He says, we'll receive the inheritance that He has promised.

There are three sections to this book:

1. **All My Single Ladies**
2. **"I's Married Na!"**
3. **Every Woman**

At the end of each chapter in the given sections, there are "Things to Consider," which summarize the chapter, and "Virtuous Assessments." The assessments are like assignments given to the reader that are typically twelve weeks in length. The reason why the duration is twelve weeks is because I have learned (especially with all of my workout routines and diet plans) that it takes twelve weeks for something to become habit forming. I would encourage you to read all sections as they all speak to being a woman. The approach taken was to identify positive resolutions to various scenarios. It's easy to revert to negative approaches and solutions. We often gravitate to what is comfortable and easy. So suggesting divorce or separation would be common and is common in our society today and sometimes the situation may require that; but this book is about learning to love and value yourself as a woman, accepting what you can't change and giving the Lord Jesus thanks in **EVERYTHING!**

It is my intention to get you to take an inward look at yourself and determine if you have been living up to the standards that God has established for Women. I will share my own personal experiences and experiences of others that help shape and change us from being silly women to virtuous women of God. I hope to capture the audiences of young and old, married and single women so that we truly understand our worth and value to the body of Christ, to society and to ourselves. So then you too can say…*"**WHO YOU CALLIN' SILLY?**"*

Part 1

All My Single Ladies

Chapter 1

Who You Callin' Silly?

Has anyone every called you silly? More than likely someone has. Due to the nature of the conversation, the comment was probably acceptable. By one definition from the online *Merriam-Webster Dictionary*, "silly" means: "Being funny in a cute way." Perhaps you did something humorous with your friends, and they thought it was silly; or when playing with a child, you made a silly face to engage the child's laughter. That's being silly.

Now, God talks about being silly as well but it's not cute. Have you ever been called silly as it relates to the context of the Bible? In another definition provided by the *Merriam-Webster Dictionary*, silly means:

> *Weak in intellect, helpless, weak; showing a lack of common sense or judgment*

God says in His word:

> *For of this sort are they which lead captive silly women, laden with sins, led away with divers lusts. Ever learning and never able to come to the knowledge of the truth. (2 Timothy 3:6)*

"Laden" means burdened; weighed down with a heavy load. So this scripture is saying men take advantage of weak, foolish women, who are in a vulnerable state from some situations in their life, which ultimately results in a woman being hurt.

Ladies...*don't be silly!*

This is not how God intends for us as women to conduct ourselves. We want the benefits and blessings of the Lord, but are we willing to sacrifice to receive those blessings? We want to do what we want, when we want and how, not adhering to any moral standards, but yet have financial gain, peace, joy and love. Are you willing to make a change to improve your life?

Chapter 2

The Realization

Making a change in your life first begins with you! You have to first recognize that you have not lived up to the potential and according to the standards that the Lord has set for you as a woman. So why then don't we have the thoughts that God has of us and recognize our worth? Not all women seek validation and acceptance from others, but some do. The realization is recognizing what is the root cause of you allowing men to use and abuse you physically and emotionally.

Our childhood experiences, coupled with the morals and values instilled in us as a child, shape who we become and what we define as acceptable behavior as we enter adulthood. How can you give something you don't have? If "tough love" was expressed in your home as a child, how can you expect to automatically display gentleness to others or your children who are in tough times? If encouragement was never given to you when you were unsuccessful at making the cheerleading team in high school, making the debate and track teams or obtaining the grade you felt you deserved, how can you encourage someone else experiencing disappointment? What if you experienced the "revolving door" friendship club of mommy's male "friends," coming to your house only for mommy and the friend to resurface a few hours later…leaving you and your siblings alone in other parts of the house (then as you became older, you understood what was occurring)? Had you gone through this, how can you respect loyalty and commitment to a man under the constitution of marriage? So then, we take what has been instilled in us as children – for eighteen-plus years – and go out into the world to practice those behaviors; often seeking for validation and acceptance of our learned behaviors, while developing our self-esteem. Most times that validation presents itself in the form of a man. He tells you how good you look, what you may have been through (because you told him first, of course, but you were so thrown off by his appearance, you totally forgot you told him your entire life story!), what he is going through and what you shouldn't accept from a man. Then here it comes...persuasion of why HE is the one for you and you fell for it. REALLY? Is this what God desires for us? Is this acceptable in the eyesight of the Lord? God does not desire for us to give in to temptation so easily and eagerly. There's no greater validation and acceptance that we can receive from another than what the Lord gives us. Listen to His validation of us:

> *I will praise You, for I am fearfully and wonderfully made; Marvelous are Your works, and that my soul knows very well. (Psalms 139:14)*

Talk about a self-esteem booster! Ladies, you are fearfully and wonderfully made! Everything God made was good and VERY good and that includes you. All that we have been through and all that we have gone through, the Lord knows, sees and yes, He cares. There is hope!

> *This I recall to my mind, therefore I have hope. Through the LORD's mercies we are not consumed, Because His compassions fail not. They are new every morning; Great*

> *is Your faithfulness. The LORD is my portion," says my soul, Therefore I hope in Him! (Lamentations 3:21-24)*

It's up to YOU to make the decision to change your life, commit to that decision and succeed because you were BORN to win!

> *But thou art he that took me out of the womb: thou didst make me hope when I was upon my mother's breasts. I was cast upon thee from the womb: thou art my God from my mother's belly. (Psalms 22:9-10)*

There's no need to be ashamed of past mistakes. We all have done something we are not proud of. The beauty of it all is that Christ accepts us as we are and forgives us. The key is YOU have to be willing to forgive yourself. There is no need to be fearful of threatening words received by a man. If you fear for your safety, you don't have to fear what a man can do to you. You may say that a person doesn't understand if they haven't experienced some form of abuse. Honey, do you really know who God is? Do you know how protective He is over his children? Not only do you have angels protecting you and keeping you – you have an almighty God, who can destroy the body and the soul, on your side, IF you're living for Him and you trust Him. These are one of the many benefits of having God on our side. He told us this:

> *The LORD is my light and my salvation; whom shall I fear? The LORD is the strength of my life; of whom shall I be afraid? When the wicked, even mine enemies and my foes, came upon me to eat up my flesh, they stumbled and fell. Though an host should encamp against me, my heart shall not fear: though war should rise against me, in this will I be confident. (Psalms 27:1-3)*

For He shall give His angels charge over you, To keep you in all your ways. (Psalms 91:11)

God's expectation is full of hope and a promising future.

For I know the thoughts that I think toward you, saith the LORD, thoughts of peace, and not of evil, to give you an expected end. (Jeremiah 29:11)

Jesus wants to give us an expected end? Yes. Our expectation is from HIM! God expects us to prosper. HE EXPECTS us to be successful. He EXPECTS us to endure temptation. He EXPECTS us to succeed! When there wasn't a God on your side and when you didn't care about yourself, God was there waiting with open arms for you to acknowledge Him and run to Him to give you the peace, joy and comfort that you sought! Instead you dried your eyes, ignored His voice (which often comes through someone He sends to give you hope) by saying you weren't ready to make a change. So, then you begin the vicious cycle all over again, hurting yourself.

It's very easy to use your situation as an excuse of why you allow yourself to be taken advantage of. I could've also used my upbringing as an excuse. My mom and dad were married before I was conceived. They wed at the age of nineteen. My mom became pregnant with me. When I was four years old, they separated and have not been together since. All throughout my life, my mother worked two jobs, making sure that I had a decent life and that she could provide for the two of us, without being reliant upon a man (she did have boyfriends but she was very particular in what I saw, whom I saw and who came by our house). Oftentimes, I'd stay with my grandmother after school along with my three other female cousins while our moms were either working other shifts or went to their second job.

The three of us were all the same age, just months apart. We had "community" involvement. My mom and grandmother made sure that I had the love and support I needed from them so that I didn't fall into the stereotype and stigma that society set for children brought up in single-parent homes. My mother NEVER spoke ill of my dad. She showed me pictures of him with us for the first four years of my life; she made me to know his birthday and even if I didn't talk to him on his birthday, I knew when it was dad's birthday. I would go to Bayou La Batre, Alabama, to visit my mom's family and Dawes, Alabama, to visit my dad's family. I would stay the summer with my dad's parents, to continue to have a connection and relationship with them and my other relatives on my dad's side. When my mom could not take me to Dawes, both she and I ensured that Grandma Annie (my dad's mother) had pictures of me as a child and of all of my children as I became an adult.

Inwardly, my mom resented how my dad did not respond to me and she knew the intimate details of why they separated, but she NEVER shared with me until I was an adult and began to ask questions. She knew how to contact him if necessary when he needed to be reminded of my birthday or if I wanted to talk to him. He would then call and make empty promises of seeing me…time after time. I recall one instance of talking to my dad and him stating he was on his way to see me. I sat in the window until late evening, waiting for him to arrive, which never occurred. I cried and my mom comforted me, often covering for him to console me. Even as a child, I did not desire to obtain gifts and toys from my dad. I simply wanted to be with him.

I love my mother for not planting a negative seed. She allowed me to form my own opinion and conclusions of my dad as I became an adult. It was then that I began to realize some of the reasons why my dad lied to me and it wasn't that he didn't love me. He liked to drink. I can't say that he was an alcoholic because I wasn't around him enough. What I can say is that every time I'd see him, from a child up through an adult (until he said he gave his life to Christ) he was always drunk or had a drink in his hand. My dad and I still don't have a relationship, for whatever reason. It's not because I have not tried on numerous occasions to reach out to him. He had remarried years ago and had three other children, whom I had a decent relationship with as well. We didn't talk often but it was on occasion. Time and years passed since I had tried to connect with him. This last time was 2005 and I was pregnant with my second child. I had heard that he had given his life to the Lord. I thought: "Yes!! We can finally have a relationship…and my children can establish a relationship with their granddad! Thank you, Lord."

He got my number and he called me (to my surprise), as I sat in the parking lot of a store, about to get out of my car. I cried and poured my heart out to him, expressing to him that I loved him, forgave him and didn't have any ill feelings. We were on a path to new beginnings. He invited me, my husband and children over to his house so they could meet his wife and children (whom, again, I had met and known over the years). At this time, my first child was two years old and I had delivered my second baby girl who was eight months old. Needless to say, I was elated. I thought, *this is it*. Finally, we have reconnected.

A few months passed and I hadn't heard from him. I stopped by his house because the phone number I had was no longer in service and I wanted to give him a calendar of my baby. She modeled for a well-known company that produced nursing products and she made the cover of the calendar for that year. When I rang the doorbell, there was no reply, so I left the calendar in his door with a note. I had soon learned that he moved to a new house in the city, not knowing if he ever received the calendar. I never knew where he moved or had any contact information. My sister who was under me (who was not the child of my dad's current wife) would often call and she and I would keep in contact. She shared with me that our dad had moved. I asked her to inform him that I had been trying to reach him, with no reply from him. At this point, I felt I was chasing him to reconnect with him, feeling as if he didn't want that. As of this writing, the relationship I desired has not come to fruition.

Every time I get pregnant, I get emotional and desire a relationship with him or begin to wonder why I was never important to him. He can't deny me. I resemble my mom but have more of his features so it wasn't a matter of questioning if I was his child. I graduated high school at sixteen, went on to college to obtain my bachelor's and master's degrees, got married, had no children outside of the institution of marriage and gave my life to Christ. I did everything according to the "American Way" (to obtain your education, marry and then build a family). So what did I do to be so undeserving of his love?

Maybe my dad doesn't know how to be a dad? Maybe the relationship I so desired with my dad would have hindered the work God had for me. Maybe I went through this to be a witness to share with someone else that they can make it! It wasn't until recently that I came to the conclusion that things happen for a reason. MY realization is that God is my Father and He has given me unconditional love, which has filled the void that was once there. I don't know why there's no relationship with my dad but it doesn't matter anymore. Throughout my life, Jesus had his hands on my life and has led me to THIS day because HE KNEW what He had instilled in me. It doesn't matter if one or both parents are in your life.

The point is WITHOUT JESUS YOU CANNOT MAKE IT! It's unfortunate, but it's my dad's loss. It will never be too late for him to establish a relationship with me but both parties have to desire that. I forgive him and I can't judge him. Only God can. But I have now moved on and accept the cards I've been dealt.

Women, listen. Do your part; don't worry about what others may or may not do for you or your children (if you have any). If the dad of your child doesn't pay child support, get family support. What does that mean? Create a loving community with your parents, siblings, cousins, aunts and uncles so your child never experiences lack of love. That child did not ask to be here but was placed here for a reason. Your blessing may come as a result of how you raise and nurture your child. Through your love and support, you are raising up a nation unto the Lord. Just through one child, a child that can change the world. You do not know what the future holds for your child. I'm sure Bill Gates's mom didn't know how influential the projects and ideas he had as a child would change how the world communicates. Oprah's mom had NO idea how her daughter would bring together women of all cultures and races. Maya Angelou's parents had no idea the gift of her words would change the way children learn in schools and the manner in which theatrical plays and shows are produced, just on the gift of a spoken word. How easy would it have been to take my situation and seek for love in a man because my dad wasn't in my life? HOW EASY OF AN EXCUSE WOULD IT HAVE BEEN?

What is your reality? Have you allowed yourself to be taken advantage of or do you take advantage of men? Do you want to stop the vicious cycles of life that have strongholds on your freedom? Are you ready to take the next step into true womanhood that's not defined by age but by the maturity of your mind?

Here's reality…Jesus is the only way to bring peace and change to YOUR reality. It must start with realizing that a change is needed in your life, for you and you only. If you do it for someone else, it won't last. Then you have to separate yourself from the negative people and environments that cause YOU harm. It's time to make YOU a priority.

> *Wherefore come out from among them, and be ye separate, saith the Lord, and touch not the unclean thing; and I will receive you. (2 Corinthians 6:17)*
>
> *Be ye not unequally yoked together with unbelievers: for what fellowship hath righteousness with unrighteousness? And what communion hath light with darkness? And what agreement hath the temple of God with idols? For ye are the temple of the living God; as God hath said, I will dwell in them, and walk in them; and I will be their God, and they shall be my people. (2 Corinthians 6:14, 16)*

You have to decide that God is first and no one or nothing else!! There has to be a fear! Yes, literally afraid that ok…if I go against the Word of God, something negative may happen and I may not be able to get back to a place where I can ask for forgiveness. You cannot play Russian roulette with your life. You only have one life to live. Why not experience the joy of life that God promised on this earth AND the world to come?

The Bible talks about how if you love Jesus, you will keep His commandments (which are things He specifically says for us to do or not to do in the Bible). The love of God constrains us from doing the wrong thing, IF you want be kept.

> *For the love of Christ constraineth us; (2 Corinthians 5:14)*

That love for Jesus and desire to not disappoint Him will overtake your desire to do wrong. You just have to say NO!!! Remember the strong desire you had to obtain the attention of the man that you never thought you'd get? Recall how you were adamant about proving people wrong who said you wouldn't amount to anything and the drive you had to prove those people wrong? Recall the dream you had to start your own business and the way you refused to let ANYONE deter you from reaching that goal?

That same intense and fierce desire to succeed in your personal life has to be strong and that much more, to live a life well-pleasing unto the Lord.

Things to Consider

Joy, love, peace, etc. are some of the fruit (not fruits) from the Spirit that we desire to attain, but it only comes through accepting Jesus as your personal savior.

> *But the fruit of the Spirit is love, joy, peace, longsuffering, gentleness, goodness, faith, Meekness, temperance: against such there is no law. (Galatians 5:22-23)*

These are the intangible things that most people seek and don't find because they don't totally surrender to change. Once you realize and accept your reality, you have to decide if that reality has held you hostage and requires a change or if you will allow that reality to continue to control your life.

Virtuous Assessment

1. Identify your reality. What event or person in your past or present has prevented you from being the beautiful, strong woman that you are?

2. Determine what you will do with your reality. Will you separate yourself or accept the hurt that you have caused (yes, you have caused because you can take your life back and have control) and continue to live with it?

3. Do what you will with your reality. If you have decided that this is it and more than enough and that it's time to move into the expectations the Lord has for you, DROP your reality…change your number, move, distance your self…BY ANY MEANS NECESSARY in the will of God. Acknowledge your transgressions to the Lord and ask Jesus for His guidance to do what He has planned for you in your life. He will direct your paths and make the way that seems impossible, straight and clear. It's time to act on faith.

   I will go before thee, and make the crooked places straight:
   I will break in pieces the gates of brass, and cut in sunder
   the bars of iron: (Isaiah 45:2)

Chapter 3

The Commitment

Once you've accepted the realities of your life and you have forgiven yourself, you can begin to make a commitment to yourself and to the Lord that you will conduct yourself like the woman God intends for you to be. That woman is to believe in who you are, along with the power you possess as a woman, and to recognize the ability to use your power! The commitment is changing to become a better you.

You can't help anyone if you don't first help yourself. When you're preparing for take-off on an airplane, the procedure explained by the flight attendant for an emergency landing is to first place the breathing mask on you and then assist others. You have to help yourself first. It begins inwardly and then displays itself outward to others. You have to be sincere with your commitment. Don't come to God because you need a "quick" change, like your rent is due or you don't have enough money to pay your bills. You're trying to use Him. Do you think God doesn't know when you're sincere? If you're not sincere with the Lord, your commitment won't last. Just as soon as that man comes back and presents something appealing to you or just as soon as things look brighter and your bills are all paid, it becomes no longer important to attend Bible Study, or everything else takes precedence over going to church to hear the Word of God. When you truly give your life to Christ, you have

NO DESIRE to go back to the things that caused you harm. In fact, Jesus said this:

> *And I give unto them eternal life; and they shall never perish; neither shall any man pluck them out of my hand. My Father, which gave them me, is greater than all; and no man is able to pluck them out of my Father's hand. (John 10:28-29)*

Here's what I've learned: there's no such thing as "backsliding" when you give your life to the Lord and you are TRULY committed to him. If you backslid, you never knew Him and never fully committed to Him because Jesus said God is greater than all, which means everyone and NO ONE is able to take you from Him! God made everything and everyone including evil. You don't think He has enough power to keep you? The question is, do you want to be kept?

How Clean is Your Temple?

You've decided to make a commitment to live for Christ. Let's begin with your body. Your temple is your body. When you make a commitment to live for the Lord, your body is no longer yours. You've expressed to the Lord that you are a living sacrifice and willing to be used by Him.

> *I beseech you therefore, brethren, by the mercies of God, that ye present your bodies a living sacrifice, holy, acceptable unto God, which is your reasonable service. (Romans 12:1)*

Reasonable service means it's not hard to do. Something that is reasonable means it's doable, it's fair and the service is our job. SO we are to present our bodies a sacrifice to be used by God, because it is a fair request and it is our obligation to do so.

Do you let men "touch" God's temple even after you've committed to live for Him? God will NOT dwell in an unclean temple. Your body is the temple of the living God. Some may say: "I have friends, but we don't have sex. We're just friends. I get along better with guys because women gossip…they are messy." Let's be honest. We're adults, right? You know what intentions you have before you do anything. If you go over a man's house or he comes by yours and you tell him: "You know I'm a Christian? We can be cool and just hang out, but nothing else." Do you think that man is listening?

Do you know what he's saying or may say to you: "I don't think the Lord would mind you having friends, would he?" Men don't even honor your beliefs in Christ because you don't. They don't honor it because with our lips we say we represent someone or something but our actions do not follow who we say we represent. Do you think that you will not begin to have stronger feelings for this man? Sure it may start off innocent – but the more you spend time with someone, the more time you want to spend.

ALL MY SINGLE LADIES….come on!!! That's being silly. You are setting yourself up. Eventually, the conversation is going to go somewhere, where it should not such as: "Why are you not with someone…what are you looking for in a man…. what do you look for in a woman?" Then, you begin having thoughts that are not pure thoughts and not in alignment with your commitment. But then YOU SAY: "We haven't done anything!" According to God's precious Word, to even LOOK at a man or woman in a lustful way, you've already sinned:

> *You have heard that it was said to those of old you shall not commit adultery. But I say to you that whoever looks at a*

> *woman to lust for her has already committed adultery with her in his heart. (Matthew 5:27-28)*

You are cheating on your husband. When you decided to give your life to Christ, you made the Lord your husband.

> *For thy Maker [is] thine husband; the LORD of hosts [is] his name; and thy Redeemer the Holy One of Israel; The God of the whole earth shall he be called. (Isaiah 54:5)*

Do you think the Lord...your husband...who provides and takes care of you, lives with you and IN you...would want ANOTHER MAN...in His house? Chileplease, don't be silly. Your body is described as a temple because the Lord wants to dwell and live within you. Once He knows that He can trust you, He will put His Spirit in you to dwell in you, lead you and guide you.

> *If any man defile the TEMPLE of God, him shall God destroy; for the TEMPLE of God is holy, which [TEMPLE] ye are. (I. Corinthians 3:17)*

> *And what agreement hath the TEMPLE of God with idols? For ye are the TEMPLE of the living God; as God hath said, I will dwell in them, and walk in [them]; and I will be their God, and they shall be my people. (2 Corinthians 6:16)*

Since your body is where God lives, what do you put in your temple? Is it clean? Do you eat healthy? Do you smoke or drink "sociably"? And you think the Lord will dwell in it? God is pure, righteous and just and He requires that of us.

> *Every word of God [is] pure: he [is] a shield unto them that put their trust in him. (Proverbs 30:5)*

> *[There is] a generation [that are] pure in their own eyes, and [yet] is not washed from their FILTHINESS. (Proverbs 30:12)*
>
> *And every man that hath this hope in him purifieth himself, even as he is pure. (I John 3:3)*

He did not make us; He gave us a choice to commit and live for Him. Be responsible for your commitment. Surely you don't want to play with the Lord. He can destroy your body and your Spirit.

> *And fear not them which kill the body; but are not able to kill the soul: but rather fear him which is able to destroy both soul and body in hell. (Matthew 10:28).*

There's an inner being living within those of us who have accepted Jesus as our personal savior. It's like being pregnant with a child. In the first trimester, you can't feel the child moving. However, all of the vital organs and body parts are being created and yet you have no idea if everything is okay inwardly with the child. You begin to notice all of the changes your body is going through internally, that give you signs that you ARE pregnant. For example, you miss your period; you also begin to experience fatigue, nausea, a mass production in saliva, possible vomiting and other symptoms, all because your body is making changes rapidly. You're still unsure if you really are pregnant (really we know, we are just in denial) so you take a test or you make an appointment with the doctor to confirm your suspicions.

This test given by the doctor determines the hormonal levels in your body which confirms or denies if you're pregnant. You then soon begin to notice changes to your body outwardly, baby movement and then finally, delivery of the child in the latter portion of the pregnancy.

So it is with the Spirit of the living God…Oh My God! Initially, you may not respond the way others do, you may not be touched like others but when you read His Word (which you don't quite understand just yet because this is all new to you) and when the Pastor brings forth the message during Sunday morning service, something touches you on the inside. You can't describe it – but you just know it wasn't there before you decided to make a commitment. So then you continue in the Word…learning about Jesus and this new way of life…this new way of thinking that you have accepted, and then you begin to feel a burning in the pit of your stomach. Something makes you want to move but you can't explain it.

> *Therefore, if anyone is in Christ, he is a new creation; old things have passed away; behold, all things have become new. (2 Corinthians 5:17)*

As you continue in this new life, you begin to hear a still, quiet voice telling you not to go that direction today or don't do this tomorrow. Outwardly, your peers begin to notice a change in your speech and appearance, and you don't "hang" out as you did before. You yearn to be in service with the congregation, desiring to know more about this Jesus. Listen. You mean to tell me we can have the Spirit of God, which formed the whole word, but yet cares enough about us to live inside of US? Yes, it is because He is concerned about your life and well-being and wants you to be successful, desires you to have peace, wants you to have joy, in so much that He desires to live in you so that He may lead you. Although you may not always be happy with the outcomes or situations in your life, you still have joy in knowing that everything is all working in your favor.

> *And we know that all things work together for good to them that love God, to them who are the called according to his purpose. (Romans 8:28)*

He loved you SO MUCH, even when you had no GOD-consciousness and could care less about reading a Bible or knowing who Jesus was, He took care of you and watched over you when you were in dangerous situations and places you had no business being. So I ask you again. Now that you made the commitment to live for Christ, do you think He wants you to put anything on the inside of you? Defiling can be described in many ways. It comes from impure thoughts of things you used to do, and places you used to go and people you used to be with.

Another form of defiling is not taking care of your body, eating and drinking anything and everything you desire, which ultimately results in sickness and disease like high blood pressure and diabetes. Ask yourself this question. Would you want to live in a place with dirty carpeting, filthy floors, unwashed clothing piled to the top of the dryer, dirty bedding, toilets with rings and pee stains on the seat, sinks with hair particles and leftover toothpaste? Feels nasty right? So how do you think God feels? Still don't think God wants to live in you? Think about this. In the Old Testament of the Bible, God spoke to his people through pillars of fire or clouds:

> *And the LORD went before them by day in a pillar of cloud to lead the way, and by night in a pillar of fire to give them light, so as to go by day and night (Exodus 13:21)*

Then it's as if He said…no, this isn't enough. They need to know that I understand what they are going through on this earth, so I'm going to send ME in the form of a physical earthly body (which is Jesus) and go through EVERYTHING they will go through so they know and see for themselves that they can live in this present evil world and not give in to temptations and evil schemes. I will not sin because there is no sin in me. It's impossible!

> *For He made Him who knew no sin to be sin for us, that we might become the righteousness of God in Him (2 Corinthians 5:21)*

And if all the sufferings that Jesus went through were not enough, it's as if God said: "Okay. They will be without excuse. I'm going to live inside of them so that I can lead them and direct them back to Me to be with Me. No one can live as close to you as I can. No one will understand like I do. I'll give you Me inside of you!" If that's not commitment then I'm confused.

Next, here come the excuses: "I'm trying to do right. God knows my heart... It's hard." Listen, I understand this is a new life and a new way of thinking, but Jesus didn't TRY to die for our sins...He did. God didn't TRY to make the world. He did! Let's be honest, who are we fooling? Certainly not yourself. You know what you are doing and what you want to do. Surely not God...He knows our thoughts before we have them.

> *You know my sitting down and my rising up; You understand my thought afar off. (Psalms 139:2)*

Here's why "I'M TRYING" doesn't work...

> *But the Lord is faithful, who will establish you and guard you from the evil one (2 Thessalonians 3:3)*

God is saying He is committed to you and He will protect you from all evil. You have to have the desire to be kept. He told us to separate ourselves and to stay clear from anything that looks evil.

> *Abstain from all appearance of evil. (I Thessalonians 5:22)*

Do we do this? We continue to be around people and things that cause harm and hurt to our lives and damage our spirit.

> *No temptation has overtaken you except such as is common to man; but God is faithful, who will not allow you to be tempted beyond what you are able, but with the temptation will also make the way of escape, that you may be able to bear it. (1 Corinthians 10:13-14)*

Even after you continue to associate with people who did the things that made you unhappy, the Lord still made a way for you to get out of it; but did you choose the escape route? Look back over every situation in your life and I guarantee you can recall being in uncompromising situations. Even still, a way was made for you to not get hurt, to not be in harm's way, to not be taken advantage of.

> *For He shall give His angels charge over you, to keep you in all your ways… (Psalms 91:11)*

> *You will keep him in perfect peace, whose mind is stayed on You, Because he trusts in You. (Isaiah 26:3)*

"I'm trying" doesn't work because the Lord will keep you. When you commit to Him, He will commit to you. Your commitment is not working because you came to the Lord with a problem, desperate and in hopeless despair. So you gave Him your problem, seeking a quick resolution. What happen to your heart? God doesn't want your problem; He wants your heart! He wants you to commit to living a life well-pleasing to Him so that your problems no longer control you. Stop giving God your problems and give Him your life.

Another form of commitment is marriage. The Lord already said that He is our Husband (spiritual), which means He will take care of our every need. He said He would supply all of our needs. Then, when He finds a woman being faithful to Him (honoring his Word, living whole heartedly for Him, being obedient to Him, putting no one else before Him, loving ourselves and respecting and genuinely loving others as well), He will grant you your desires, by blessing you with a husband, if that is your desire. Let's be honest. Most single women desire to be married. But are you a wife yet? Before you can be a wife to a man of God, you have to be a wife to the Lord. How? If and when the Lord finds you faithful to HIM...taking care of your responsibilities and putting Him first...HE will reward you openly.

> *That thine alms may be in secret: and thy Father which seeth in secret himself shall reward thee openly. (Matthew 6:4)*

Think about this. You are asking God to give you HIS SON and asking Jesus for one of His brothers. I'm assuming that if you desire a man, he is a man of God, since you are now committed to Christ and I'm certain that your desires are to someone who would share your beliefs, right?

1. A son honors His Father....

   > *My son, if thou wilt receive my words, and hide my commandments with thee; So that thou incline thine ear unto wisdom, and apply thine heart to understanding (Proverbs 2:1-2)*

2. A son obeys and listens to His Father...

My son, keep my words, and lay up my commandments with thee. Keep my commandments, and live; and my law as the apple of thine eye. (Proverbs 7:1-2)

3. A son is an extension of his father...

And God said; Let us make man in our image, after our likeness: and let them have dominion over the fish of the sea, and over the fowl of the air, and over the cattle, and over all the earth, and over every creeping thing that creepeth upon the earth. So God created man in his own image, in the image of God created he him... (Genesis 1:26-27)

So now you're asking the Lord to give you one of His sons. The Lord needs to know you will take care of his son, guide the house, take care of the children, be a help in every area and more importantly still keep Him (the Lord) first. If you haven't been a wife to the Lord, do you believe He's ready to give you one of his sons?

Ladies, if you confess Christ as your personal Savior and a man is able to deter you and make you give in to temptation, ultimately going against the Word of God, that means you cheated on the Lord. If you cheat on the Lord, do you think a man of God will believe that you can remain faithful unto Him? Are you certain you're ready to be a wife to one of God's sons?

As a single lady and a wife unto the Lord, ask yourself these few simple questions:

- Do you wash clothes weekly or do you wait for them to pile up?
- Do you buy detergent to last for some time or do you wait until you run out?

- Do you stock up on toiletries (i.e. tissue, paper towel, soap, toothpaste) to last for a month or through the winter months?
- How often do you mop your floors?
- Do you clean out the inside and outside of your microwave and refrigerator/freezer?
- Do you study God's word? To show yourself approved unto Him and not to others to prove you have the ability to quote EVERY scripture in the Bible?
- Do you represent Christ everywhere you go or just at Sunday morning service? In other words, if someone saw you out in the workplace or out performing your daily routine, could they recognize something different about you? Would they be shocked to see you walking through the church doors or singing in the choir because you're a chameleon and you change based on the environment you're in?
- Do you pay your bills on time or do you use the grace period? You DO realize your credit is important right? You say you're representing Christ. Do you think God would be pleased with disconnection notices and large credit card debts because you impulse shop and do not take care of what's important first?
- Do you clean door handles, dresser drawer handles or the handle used to flush the toilet?
- Do you soak and clean the combs and brushes you used to do your hair?

If You Have Children:

- Do you explain to your children how to wash up in the bath tub as you are washing them?

- Do you teach your children how to iron their clothing and plan their outfits for the entire week or are you scrambling to find their clothes in the morning when they wake up for school?
- Do you teach them to not only brush their teeth, but also brush their tongue AND floss?
- Do you change toothbrushes every six months (or less)?
- Do your children have annual and semiannual visits to the dentist and doctor offices?
- Do you wash down your walls and doors (kids are at school all day with others and germs spread...we are still talking about being a wife and keeping a clean temple)?
- Do you plan your weekly meals and buy food to cook meals for you or your children or do you make your children eat ramen noodles, cereal, chips or fast food because you didn't plan?
- Do you show and teach your children how to clean the house?
- If you've committed to Christ, do you teach your children what God says and what living a life pleasing to the Lord means?
- Do your children understand prayer, why we pray and how to pray?
- Do you teach your children scriptures and review the Sunday School lesson with them?
- Do you leave your under-aged children at home alone, unattended by an adult?
- Do you allow them to help you clean (like folding clothes, vacuuming, cleaning their room, making their bed, cleaning windows) and if they don't do it according to your standards, do you teach them how to or do you yell and reprimand them because they did it "wrong"?

- Do you explain why the chore was done incorrectly? Jesus was loving and kind. If we say we have characteristics like Him, shouldn't we portray those same characteristics of loving-kindness?
- Do you teach them how to be responsible and take care of their belongings?
- Do you wash you and your kid's sheets and bedding or do you wait until they are so unclean, you have to throw them away and buy new ones?
- Do you wash your children's white tennis shoes in bleach and let them air dry to keep them looking clean and lasting a little longer?
- Do you wash the coats and hats?
- Do you look through your children's book bags and review their homework with them daily?
- Does your child's teacher know you and view your relationship as a partnership to educate your child, or does the teacher cringe at your appearance because you always take sides with your child?
- Do you just take the time to simply say I love you? Or do you treat them unfairly because you and their dad did not have a lasting relationship?

Since we are talking about children, let's make sure, ladies, that we understand who children really are and what they mean to the Lord. You DO realize that the children are not yours right? God said:

Behold, all souls are Mine; The soul of the father As well as the soul of the son is Mine; (Ezekiel 18:4)

Isn't it amazing how the child carries the parents' genetic makeup, characteristics and mannerisms but they are not ours?

The Lord trusted us enough to have children and bring them up as respectable and God-fearing. Who are we to abuse a helpless child or put that child in harm's way? Please don't be silly!

Just when you think no one is watching, when you leave the child in the basement in the dark because that's your harsh way of reprimanding, or when you will not allow the child to eat because that's your harsh way of reprimanding…God sees everything. Or what about when you have abandoned your child and leave the child with anyone or anywhere for your own pleasure? And you wonder why your needs are not being met? You wonder why you're having so many ailments in your body?

Oh God, you will reap what you sow. Children are God's reward. How you treat them, what you do to them and what you allow others to do to them will get you in trouble. You WILL be responsible because God will hold you accountable and you will suffer.

Some women may say: "I didn't want children. It was a one-night stand before I committed to living for Jesus Christ." Even still, there was a reason why God saw fit for you to have a child, for His good pleasure. Not for your own pleasure.

We're talking about something that's a part of you, that you carried for nine months…the child ate what you ate…heard the words you spoke…read what you read…slept when you slept…you began raising that child in your womb BEFORE birth and you can't show love? Even if you weren't shown love as a child, how about breaking that curse and cycle, by starting with your own child?

This is a small list of things you do to being committed, keeping your temple clean, and being a wife unto the Lord. Let's hold true to our commitment. The Lord was committed to loving us and proving His love for us. Will you commit to Him? Have you wholeheartedly committed to Him?

Things to Consider

Making a commitment to anyone or anything means that you are being truthful and honest with yourself. A commitment to Jesus Christ should not be taken lightly and must be sincere. One person we cannot fool is Jesus. He knows what we are thinking before we think it. Even if you desire to make a commitment and you believe Jesus is real, but you are scared and uncertain of the unknown, ask Him to help you. Even the disciples told Jesus they believe but help their unbelief. Help you to believe what seems to be impossible, to change your thought process to be more Christ-like. A lifelong change doesn't occur overnight. Just like you put on your clothes in layers and you remove them layer by layer, as you begin to learn about the Lord and grow in Him, you "take off" things that make you go against the Word of God. Listen, that doesn't mean that you accept the Lord as your Savior and then continue to smoke and say the Lord knows my heart. NO. You make the effort NOT to indulge. If you want the Lord's results, He requires your effort. What does that mean? FAITH! You can't please Him without it!

Virtuous Assessment

1. Draw closer to God and He will draw closer to you. Take the opportunity to read at least fifteen minutes a day. Start with the New Testament and learn the works of Jesus, beginning with the Book of Matthew and onward. I guarantee that fifteen minutes will turn into thirty minutes or an hour as you learn of Him and who Jesus really is.

Submit yourselves therefore to God. Resist the devil, and he will flee from you. Draw nigh to God, and he will draw nigh to you. Cleanse your hands, ye sinners; and purify your hearts, ye double minded. (James 4:7-8)

2. Trust God with your heart, mind and soul. Even when you don't know who to trust and you're afraid, don't doubt Him. Jesus is REAL and He desires the best for us.

   Trust in the LORD with all thine heart; and lean not unto thine own understanding. In all thy ways acknowledge him, and he shall direct thy paths. (Proverbs 3:4-5)

3. For three months, submit totally unto the Lord without fear, doubt and reservation. Establish a relationship with Him as you would with a man you desire to become acquainted with. Talk to Him throughout your day, learn of Him, attend Bible Study and not just Sunday morning service (when most people attend), pray to Him, thank Him (for EVERY situation) and watch your commitment become your NEW reality!

Chapter 4

Love

With commitment comes love. Do you love yourself, your parents or your children? The most common reply is yes. When you love someone or something you don't want to hurt it or see it hurt. Jesus said:

> *But God, who is rich in mercy, because of His great love with which He loved us, even when we were dead in sins, made us alive together with Christ (by grace you have been saved). (Ephesians 2:4)*

> *But God demonstrates His own love toward us, in that while we were still sinners, Christ died for us. (Romans 5:8)*

> *The LORD has appeared of old to me, saying: "Yes, I have loved you with an everlasting love; Therefore with loving-kindness I have drawn you. (Jeremiah 31:3)*

Some don't truly understand love and what it means to be loved and give love. What many think is love is really just a form of selfishness, not pure love. Selfishness can be thought as this:

> *I love you because of the way you make me feel.*
>
> *I love you because of what you do for me.*
>
> *I love you because of what I can get from you.*
>
> *I love you because of how you make me look.*

When the feeling is gone, the money runs low and the "no one makes me feel like you do" has fizzled, the love is gone and finds refuge elsewhere. That's not love, ladies. However, TRUE love can be identified when we think like this:

> *I love you because you are valuable and precious.*
>
> *I love you because I want the best for you.*
>
> *I love you because of who you are and just the way you are.*
>
> *I love you (Jesus) because you first loved me.*
>
> *I love you (Jesus) because there is no me without you.*
>
> *I love you (Jesus) because when I didn't know what sin was, you sacrificed your life so I could have a better life.*

Jesus put it best:

> *The greatest love you can show is to give your life for your friends. (John. 15:13)*

How unselfish was the act of Jesus? Jesus, you did this for me? You gave your life, died for me, when I didn't acknowledge you or even care about all the sufferings you had gone through just for me? A human giving their life to the point of death has to be the most unselfish act of love. There's no way that the motives of Jesus were a result of any benefit that He would receive. Would any of the men you are using for selfish gain give their lives for you?

When we were so self-absorbed and could care less who we hurt in our paths, as long as we got what we needed…during that time, God STILL loved us! While we were YET sinners.

> *But God commendeth his love toward us, in that, while we were yet sinners, Christ died for us. (Romans 5:8)*

Still not convinced that He loved you and loves you despite all that you've done? Let's look at just how much the Lord loves women. To do that, we must go back to the beginning.

> *And the LORD God caused a deep sleep to fall upon Adam, and he slept: and he took one of his ribs, and closed up the flesh instead thereof; And the rib, which the LORD God had taken from man, made he a woman, and brought her unto the man. And Adam said, This is now bone of my bones, and flesh of my flesh: she shall be called Woman, because she was taken out of Man. (Genesis 2:21-23)*

Let's discuss the ribs in the human body and its function. The rib bone is strong. Have you ever eaten beef or pork ribs? Or have you ever seen a rib bone? In the human body, the purpose of the rib cage is to provide protection to vital organs. Vital means these organs are imperative to living. Without them functioning we cannot live. Did you know that the primary vital organs which are protected are the heart and the lungs? The lungs allow us to take in oxygen so we can breathe. The heart provides oxygen and blood flow to the rest of the body (honey if the heart doesn't pump, we don't live). Not only do the ribs protect these organs, they also provide the main support for the entire skeletal system, which simply means providing support so that all the bones fitly join together in the body, as God created.

Now let's get an understanding of this. According to the scripture just quoted in Genesis 2:21-23, the Lord caused Adam to fall asleep and He took one of his ribs, and made a woman. Do you understand why He made us from the rib? God wanted us to be strong so that we would be able to endure all that we would have to AS a woman! Women are the vital support of the family structure that holds the family together. When it all seems to be falling apart, a woman can pull it together. And you often wondered when you were growing up, how your mother could work from nine to five (sometimes overtime), raise a family, cook and clean and help provide for a household? THAT'S WHO WE ARE! You mean to tell me, as a woman, I am critical to this structure of life? I am VITAL to the creation of this world? YES!!! It's the man that plants the "seed" but ladies, we bring forth the fruit. There would be no populating this world without us!

Have you ever heard a married couple talking and the man speaks about how the woman may have left the children with him for a moment to maybe run errands and when she returns he says he doesn't know how she does it all? Sweetheart let me tell you. It's what we are made of. We ARE the rib…born to be strong, supportive, nurturing, well-rounded! It's typically the woman who teaches that child its first words, letters, shapes and colors. It is the woman that teaches that child right from wrong. The man reinforces what we have taught, but that woman instills the values and beliefs that she and her husband share. On top of all this, having the ability to bring forth a child, from within our own bodies, watching our bodies transform, stretch and maneuver to have ANOTHER being come out of you? Ladies, listen, men are strong but honey, if a man had to have a child, the abortion rate would be AT LEAST 95%! There's an emotional strength and connection that only a woman has to nurture a child while it's still in the womb.

While the rib cannot be seen from the outside of the body, it holds a major function on the inside. While most people don't see what we as women do on a daily basis in the home, you better believe it's known outside of the home in how you as a woman conduct yourself in the workplace, or when your children are receiving amazing compliments of respect and leadership during their school conferences and how well kept they are. Sometimes the fights and the struggles women go through are unseen as we smile and hold it all together, saying a quick prayer to the Lord: "Lord please help me. I don't know how I will manage." And He's right there all along and you're making it all along. So from this day forward, do not allow someone to tell you you're weak minded, you're not strong, you won't make it, you'll never be anything. You ARE somebody in Jesus. You ARE strong. You can do ALL things through Christ, who gives you the strength.

There is another side to this rib thing though. Again, within the human body, the rib cage is also one of the most difficult structures to treat…even if just one rib from the rib cage gets damaged, the entire body suffers. So it is with a woman. If we become broken in heart, from physical and emotional abuse, betrayal or deceit, the family suffers dreadfully. It's so difficult to mend and repair the heart of a woman because when the trust is gone, everything else disintegrates. When a woman loves, she gives all that she has and trusts that man with her whole heart. Why not put the time and effort we put into loving a man and desiring the attention of a man into getting the attention of our Father? Women, it's important to not trust people, you trust the God that lives IN that person, if they are God-fearing. You love people but you don't trust them. I love my husband and thank God for him daily. But he is made from the dirt of the ground. He is flesh and if he doesn't bring his flesh under subjection as we all have to, he will give in to temptation. But I do trust the God that lives in him because his delight is in the Word of the Lord and he puts God first in everything. As long as we keep God first, we obtain the favor of God. God said in His word:

> *Put not your trust in princes, nor in the son of man, in whom there is no help. (Psalms 146:3)*
>
> *Thus says the LORD: Cursed is the man who trusts in man and makes flesh his strength, whose heart departs from the LORD. (Jeremiah 17:5)*

Only God can mend a broken heart and remove all guilt and shame. Only He can fix what once was broken and repair a situation that seems irreplaceable and irreparable, then make you feel and become new.

> *He healeth the broken in heart, and bindeth up their wounds. (Psalms 147:3)*
>
> *The LORD is near to those who have a broken heart, and saves such as have a contrite spirit. (Psalms 34:18)*

Things to Consider

It's hard to break a rib. It takes a lot of effort, time and force! God loved us enough to make us JUST THAT strong because

He knew the expectations He had of us and what was required to meet those expectations in raising a nation unto him. Then, He loved us when we didn't understand love as we thought. There's no greater love than the love of Christ. So do you really love yourself to know and value your worth? You are strong and you are worth every beautiful element and bone the Lord created in you.

Virtuous Assessment

1. Have you given your life to Christ because of what He can do for you or because of what He means to you? Review your love. Is it selfish or unselfish?

2. If you've found your love of Jesus to be selfish, ask Him for forgiveness.

3. Study for three months the love of Christ and how he loved us. Look up the word "love" in your Bible's index and take each day to research a scripture and the references of how Jesus loves us, and how that love has been demonstrated and how he expects us to demonstrate love.

Chapter 5

So Just What is a Silly Woman?

As we conclude the single ladies section of this book, I thought it would be good to give you some examples of how women we may have heard about have had "silly" potential and how they handled their situations.

The Daughter of Herodias

There was a man named King Herod, also known as Herod Antipas. He was made King of Galilee. He married a woman named Herodias, who by chance, happened to be his niece AND his brother's wife. Herodias and her daughter left her uncle/husband in Rome and married King Herod. During this time, Jesus had not openly began his ministry. His time had not come, so John the Baptist's fame was known abroad as he spoke of the coming of Jesus Christ and continued to beckon for people to repent and be baptized. King Herod feared John because he knew that John was a just and holy man of God. The fear could be viewed as respect. John the Baptist heard of King Herod's marriage to Herodias and told them the truth. He told them their marriage was not lawful in the sight of God. Herodias became angry with John the Baptist, insomuch that she wanted him dead. For the time being, she had him put in prison, as she plotted. Well, her opportunity came as her husband held a birthday dinner for himself and invited all of the "who's who" to join him. Herodias persuaded her own daughter to dance provocatively in front of her stepdad/great uncle. Apparently Herodias's plan worked. The daughter's dance pleased Herod and the attendees so much, that he told his stepdaughter that she could have anything she requested and he would honor it. She consulted with her mother and the request was to have John the Baptist's head. Well, as before stated, King Herod respected John the Baptist, so when he heard this request he was sorrowful, but he honored the request because he swore in front of his acquaintances, family and friends that she could have what she wanted.

Who was silly here? To me, all three of them were silly, but since we're talking about single ladies, we will discuss the stepdaughter. Really? Come on, lady. The Bible doesn't state how old she was, but apparently she was old enough to use her sexuality to provoke the men at the dinner to give her what she desired. Women, we should never coerce our children (who once again don't belong to us) to do the wrong thing. Whether that be using their name for utility bills because your credit is destroyed, exploiting them sexually, or fulfilling a dream that you once had and making YOUR dream become your child's dream.

Of course, God's will had to be done. As John's work was completing, it was time for our Savior, Jesus Christ, to begin his ministry. But what if the daughter would have stood on the Word of God? NEVER be ashamed to stand for the truth, regardless of who it may hurt. Even if it's your own mother! The Bible says you shall know the truth and the truth shall make you free. The word "shall" is a promise! That means God will do it! One thing we know is God is not like us. He cannot and He will not lie for anyone or anything. If He said it, He's going to fulfill it.

Delilah

Let's take a look at the infamous Delilah. There was a man in the Bible by the name of Samson. Before his birth, his mom was unable to bear children and was known as barren. An angel appeared to her and foretold her how she should carry throughout her pregnancy (as far as what not to eat or drink). He also told her that she would have a son and to raise Him unto the Lord and to never allow his hair to be cut, as He would begin the process to deliver the children of Israel, God's chosen people, from the Philistines. As Samson was amidst his travels, he met a woman by the name of Delilah. Now, before Delilah, Samson was married to a woman, and that didn't work out. So then he slept with some prostitutes and met Delilah along his travels. The Bible says he loved Delilah. They were not married.

Delilah was a Philistine. But Samson was supposed to begin delivering the Israelites from the Philistines. Throughout his life, Samson and the Philistines had numerous run-ins, with him always defeating them. They were baffled at his strength and how he could defeat so many by the strength of his own hands; but what perfect opportunity. The elders of the Philistines knew that Delilah was dating Samson and told her they would each give her a large sum of money if she would find out what Samson's strength was. They even played a guilt trip on her, stating how could she not help save her own kind from their biggest enemy, Samson. This lady obviously was not in love with Samson so she agreed. Delilah asks Samson three times, with the first two times, him telling her something that was not true and then she tried these things on him only to learn he was lying. Samson was silly, too. If someone keeps asking you questions and then when you tell them something, they try on you the VERY thing that is supposed to harm you and then call your enemies to take hold of you, don't you think that person is NOT in your best interest? Since, we're talking about silly women, we won't go there. I guess Samson loved Delilah sooo much, the third and final time, as he lay in her lap, Samson told Delilah that his strength was in his hair and he would lose his strength if shaven. Thus his enemy, the Philistines, took hold of him, shaved his hair and had him in their custody. In case you didn't know, Satan will NEVER defeat God. Understand this: God created Satan and he can only do what God allows and what we allow him to do to us because God gave us the power to defeat Satan, a power we can access when we live for the Lord. Samson's hair began to grow as he was in the custody of the Philistines. While they were planning a huge sporting event with all of their people in the stadium, where Samson would be put on display, he was praying to the Lord to give him strength again. The Lord answered Samson's prayer and he killed more Philistines (including himself) through his death as he brought down the pillars of that stadium than throughout all his life. Who knows if Delilah was there, and she could have very well been, but was the money worth it?

How was Delilah silly? Women, how many times have you used a man for your own personal gain? Were you happy? For the moment the need was met, but I guarantee you that you were not happy and that same need to pay your rent, car note or cell phone bill was coming around the next month. Do you think this man will take you seriously as "wife" material? We just talked about pure love and we know it's not selfish. How does it make you feel when you learn that you're being used? What if the manager on your job asks for you to complete a task that could potentially provide you with a promotion or upgrade in pay, only to learn that you didn't receive the credit and someone else received the promotion because their "organizational" skills seemed to be more polished at that point, which is what your management team needs now? Would you feel used? Don't think you won't reap what you have sown. Just as you are using that man, he is using you as well and doing what YOU allow him to. A man can only do what you allow and if you show no respect for yourself, you cannot possibly expect him to respect you. It's not okay to be used in such a way that is not ordained by God. You're not happy and you don't have joy. You are worth so much more than the price of selling yourself short to a man when the Man Jesus owns EVERYTHING and can supply ALL of your needs. He told us that:

> *But my God shall supply all your need according to his riches in glory by Christ Jesus. (Philippians 4:19)*

He wants you to depend on HIM! That man can die on you or get married…but not to YOU. Then what will you do? Find another? Then Jesus said this:

> *Beloved, I wish above all things that thou mayest prosper and be in health, even as thy soul prospereth (3 John 1:2)*

The Lord wants us to prosper and have a good life here on earth as well. We know we will be without worry when this life ends, but prospering here means doing it according to the Word of God and all in alignment with His plans. Prosperous means financially, physically and spiritually. Short-term prosperity, while you hurt others in the process, is not prospering…it's being silly!

I Was Silly, Too!

I was once silly. I was SO intelligent that I was stupid. I knew before I even entered high school what I aspired to do, which was have a career in information technology; I was fascinated with computers. At age sixteen, I graduated from Pulaski High School, top ten percent of my class. I had made up in my mind that there were no other options for me other than college. I wanted to obtain a degree and be solely independent, not dependent on anyone but myself. That is what my mother instilled in me. She told me to never need anyone but Jesus!

You see, I grew up in church and was considered the church girl up through my early teens. In fact, my mom and dad were consistent in attending church services and practicing the principles of God through the Word of God, when I was conceived. However, when they separated, so did their commitment to Christ. Therefore, I would go to church with my granny (my mother's mother). I was her church buddy. Then, when my cousins and I would get together at granny's house while our parents were at work, we would play church and imitate everyone at church, including granny. My cousin Pookie (as we called him) would be the Pastor some times. We would sing choir songs, pretend to pass out on the floor, speak in unknown tongues (or at least try to repeat what we heard) and shout and scream until granny would tell us to quiet down. My granny was a member of Lively Stone Deliverance. They called my granny "Mother Moore." Mother Moore was known for making her sweet potato pies and zucchini bread. Granny had this song she would sing:

> "Walk on walker, talk on talker, I know you're gonna talk about me. But the more you walk and the more you talk, I know the Lord is going to take care of me…"

We would sing that song like granny. Then at night, granny had her long prayer she would pray. She would pray for everyone by name. Mind you she had eleven children. Then those who were not her children, when she couldn't remember their name, she would say: "Lord bless, them one by one and name by name." Oftentimes, she would fall asleep on her knees praying. So after a while, she would just pray in bed and when we stayed the night, best believe we were praying too…or at least listening.

I completed elementary school and then started middle school at Samuel Morse Middle School and was there from sixth to seventh grade. My mom then decided she needed a change and wanted to move out of state. My mom and I moved from Milwaukee to Little Rock, Arkansas, when I was thirteen. Most times, when you reach seventh and eighth grade, you begin to develop long friendships, you begin to like school and you become more social. So when my mom decided to move, I was distraught and wouldn't even give Little Rock a chance at first. We visited churches but none that we visited I liked. The biggest turnoff was to see people going into the church to hear the Word that could change their lives, and then before they even left the grounds of the building, they were smoking cigarettes on the steps of the entrance. So I lost my focus on Christ. I did not like Little Rock. It was so different from Milwaukee.

I attended Mabelvale Junior High School where I absorbed myself in numerous activities like National Honor Society, cheerleading and basketball to fit in and learn the southern way of living. My mom allowed me to come back to Milwaukee for the summers and I stayed with my cousin. One summer I asked if I could stay in Milwaukee for good and my aunt Ellen said I could live with her. My mom agreed and I was back in Milwaukee. I was so excited to be reunited with my family and have the opportunity to reconnect with middle school friends who had since begun high school.

A few months later, my mom moved back to Milwaukee as well and everything was complete again for me. I finished high school in Milwaukee and attended the University of Wisconsin-Milwaukee for my Bachelor's of Business Administration (BBA) with an emphasis in MIS (Management Information Systems). College was an adjustment for me. By the time college began the summer of 1992, I turned seventeen and I was still a virgin. Surrounded by young women who were older and experienced with intimacy, I felt somewhat intimidated so I avoided conversations about sex. If they did come up, I replied as if I knew what they were talking about so it didn't seem as if I wasn't sexually active. But the very thought of sex at that age just turned me off. To imagine someone else's bodily fluids entering me was just nasty. Surely, I have mine every day PLUS an extra burst of bodily fluids on a monthly basis I have to deal with; and on top of ALL that, then I'd have to deal with yours and only God knows where you been? UGH!

Don't get me wrong, I liked boys and found them attractive but they weren't my focus and that picture was just not appealing. I was taught that boys and babies didn't mix and they will always be there but the opportunity to get my degree and start a career may not be, so I listened. My walk with Christ did not exist. I didn't backslide; I never slid in. I had a zeal (a desire to learn of Him and the knowledge that Jesus did exist and was real) but I had not yet come to know Jesus for myself and what it meant to live for Him. I was interested in the Word of God as a youth but I didn't and could not have known Jesus as I do now because I would have never left Him.

That first year of college passed and I decided to take on a summer job. I didn't have to because I received academic scholarships and grants since my mother was a single parent. That covered all of my schooling; however, working was something to keep me from being idle during the summer and it taught me how to earn my own money, appreciate it and not be careless with it because I did work for it. I decided to obtain employment at a check-cashing place, where one of my older cousins was a manager and where I also met this guy. He was a little older than I and was home from the Navy. He was also my first boyfriend and the man I lost my virginity to. My mother and I were close. She established with me all throughout my life that she wanted me to feel comfortable talking to her about anything. She reassured me that I did not have to give in to peer pressure and that I could confide in her about anything. That constantly rang in my head as I grew up and as she continued to send subtle reminders that she would always be there for me. So, when I felt that this guy was worth me losing my virginity (I was now 19) I confided in her. Not that I really wanted to do it; I felt that he had been patient and waited and I at least owed him that. How often do young ladies get a subtle pressure from a guy and feel obligated to give up their virginity because "he waited"? So, I told my mom. Again, neither I nor my mom was living for Christ. She took me to the doctor to get birth control, told me the do's and dont's and to make sure he was wearing protection. She also told me to follow the rules of birth control which were to wait for thirty days for it to get into my system. So, I did. Mom and I were so close, that after the "hoorah" was over, I called her and said: "Mom, I'm done." HA HA HA! She asked if I was okay and I expressed to her that I could have stayed a virgin. HA HA HA HA!!!! Is THIS what everyone was RAVING over? UGH! Reaaallllyy? I was NOT impressed. I stayed in a relationship with this guy for two years, only to learn that he was messing around with a young lady he had been with before he entered the Navy. That was my cue to move on. So here I was introduced to this emotional rollercoaster of intimacy (which I did not enjoy) along with heartbreak and the stress of college.

    Normally when you experience heartbreak, you meet someone right away…on the rebound…and here begins my silly woman story. This guy I also met at a different job. He was not my "type" at all, but he was kind and soft-spoken. He was six years my senior, mature (so I thought) and established. He often talked about things he was going through with his baby's momma and of course I opened up about my hurtful relationship. We always met up after work, never at his house, always driving around or at my house. Come to find out, he and his child and the mother of the child lived together but he claimed they were not doing well and she was moving out of town. My mom did not like him. There were all kind of red flags that she saw because she knew "the game," but I was naïve. I resented my mom's thoughts. I just knew I had found my husband and this is who I would be with after college. We were in a relationship for two and a half years years until one day, he told me he was getting married AND she was pregnant. He claimed he was asleep and she started being intimate with him while he was asleep. Really? And you just woke up in the midst and bingo bango…YOU HAD NO IDEA??? I was so smart, I was stupid. How silly was I?

    I was very hurt. Even after this dude got married and I graduated from college, he still kept calling. He said he couldn't see why we couldn't be friends. DUDE…ARE YOU SERIOUS??? REALLY? I was so upset with myself to be SO IGNORANT. I changed all my numbers but couldn't change my work number, and at that time my phone didn't have caller ID. So I would have to answer and hear his voice on the other end. It was like rotten meat…just spoiled and stinky. I thank God for the day I got a new job with a different company because I no longer had to avoid his calls; but it was through this situation that I was drawn to Christ. I was just tired. Although it had only been two relationships, they ended in heartbreak. One I couldn't understand why and the other I was just SUPER SILLY!

    I recall sitting in the car of my rebound boyfriend, after he had gotten married and after I had graduated college. I had begun to attend church but was only a Sunday goer and had not joined the church. This was not Lively Stone Deliverance, this was a new church…Unity Gospel House of Prayer. As I sat in his car, I looked in the sky and said: "I can't do this!" Unknowingly, I said it aloud. He asked, "What did you say?" and I repeated it. That was it! I could not be stupid anymore. I was ashamed, embarrassed of myself, not proud of myself for just not recognizing the game. But it was all a part of the plan. On February 15, 1998, I dedicated my life to Christ. I gave Him my hand and not just my problems. I had NO DESIRE to even look at a man. I wanted to truly learn about the Lord, to start over and to learn myself. Yes, it was God's plan. He needed my undivided attention. He needed me to focus solely on him so He could get the glory out of my life and not to be distracted by a man.

Sure there were advances in the church from single men, but honey please, I would smile and keep moving. I had no time for mess. I had a college degree, was in school for my master's degree, had my own place and a career, but I had no peace. Before I completely surrendered, I was cursed. It was here, at Unity Gospel House of Prayer (a.k.a. UGHOP), four years later, where I would meet my husband and I soon understood although I experienced heartbreak in the world, I was being set up for success in the Lord! The Lord completed me. He made me a wife unto Him FIRST and found me being faithful to Him, so that a man, my husband, could find me…his good thing, ladies… and we obtain much favor from God!

I thank God for my silly moments. It's through those times that I can witness to other young ladies who struggle with doing the right thing and not being pressured into going against morals and standards instilled as a child and the principles of God. It's through those trials that I learned patience with God. It's through those tests that I learned how to be a woman of

God. Through it all I learned how a silly single woman becomes a virtuous woman and wife to the Lord. God said in His word, He has no respect of person. That means He doesn't care who you are and what title you possess. If He could do it for me, He can certainly do it for you. Single ladies, recognize your reality, accept what silly mistakes you may have made, and forgive yourself. Then make a commitment to change for the better for YOU! With that commitment, learn to love God with your whole heart, mind, soul and all your strength and love yourself as well. You too, then can turn silliness into virtuousness.

Part 2

"I's Married Na!"

Chapter 6

Vows

Most of us have seen the movie *The Color Purple,* based on the book written by Alice Walker. The film tells the story of a young African-American girl named Celie and shows the problems African-American women faced including poverty, racism and sexism. Miss Celie marries an older widower (Mr. Johnson) who initially showed interest in her younger sister Nettie as they frequently "observed" each other at church services. Mr. Johnson decided to ask the sisters' dad if he could have Nettie's hand in marriage. Their dad angrily rejects the proposal but offers Miss Celie. Mr. Johnson agrees and Miss Celie immediately inherits three young children from her new husband. As the children grow older, one of Miss Celie's step sons, Harpo, finds love in Miss Sofia (a role played by Oprah Winfrey), who becomes one of two women to begin Miss Celie's transformation as she finds her self-worth. At the end of the wedding ceremony of Harpo and Sofia, her friends immediately whisk her away as she proudly proclaims: "I's married na!"

Do you remember your wedding day? Regardless of how big or small, in front of a large audience or at the courthouse downtown, how beautiful was the day you exchanged vows with your husband. Everything may have not gone perfectly on the wedding day itself, but the most important thing within the ceremony were the vows and commitment made to your spouse. As you gazed into each other's eyes, suddenly everyone else in the room disappeared and it felt as if he and you were left alone to swear that you would forever take care of each other regardless of the condition of road that you would travel. For most of us, the traditional vows read:

For the future spouse:

> *"I, (Sarah/James), take you (Sarah/James), to be my (wife/husband), to have and behold from this day on, for better or for worse, for richer, for poorer, in sickness and in health, to love and to cherish, until death do us part."*

You said "I do," kissed each other, and were presented to the wedding attendants as Mr. and Mrs. "John Doe." That day was like a fairytale, as you greeted family and friends, everyone smiling and in awe of your special day. You took pictures with the wedding party (if you chose to have one) and continued the celebration at the reception with more love, food, gifts and time spent with those you cherished most to take part in your happily ever after. Some of you left the reception and went off to your honeymoon, as you continued to live in wedding bliss and fantasyland. Whether you selected the traditional vows or decided to create your own, did you really understand the vows given?

Of course you did. If you created your own, your response to the question just asked would be: "I wrote them, why is it that I wouldn't understand them?" If they were traditional, you may say: "I've heard them countless times at other weddings and my own. It simply means we will take care of each other and be there for one another regardless." To whom did you make your vows? Let's ensure that we understand the constitution of marriage. God said:

> *And the LORD God said, It is not good that the man should be alone; I will make him an help meet for him. (Genesis 2:18)*

God made Adam and all living things. As Adam slept, God formed Eve from Adam's rib (we discussed the rib in the single ladies section of this book). God saw that Adam needed a help meet. What does "help meet" mean? Let's break down this phrase.

What does "help" mean? According to the *Merriam-Webster* online dictionary help means: "to give assistance or support to." Also, according to the same dictionary, one definition of meet means: "to provide for." So here God is saying He made Adam someone who would understand him, because she came from him (his rib) and she (Eve) would give Adam assistance and support to provide for the two of them, also known as…the wife.

So as wives, we are to assist our husbands as they provide for our household. Help doesn't mean take over and help certainly does not mean be taken advantage of. It's an agreement between two to make your lives more fulfilling. God must have seen that Adam needed a companion. He had made all the animals and named them. All the animals MUST have had a "help meet" because the Word of God said there was no help meet found for Adam. God was concerned enough to see that Adam could not do this alone. He needed somebody. After Eve was formed, this is what the Word of God says:

> *And the rib, which the LORD God had taken from man, made he a woman, and brought her unto the man. And Adam said, this is now bone of my bones, and flesh of my flesh: she shall be called Woman, because she was taken out of Man.*

> *Therefore shall a man leave his father and his mother, and shall cleave unto his wife: and they shall be one flesh. (Genesis 2:22-24)*

God made Adam a wife! Even with God making Adam a wife and bringing Eve to him, they still had problems. They did not keep their vow to the Lord. The Lord gave Adam a commandment to NOT eat of the tree of knowledge of good and evil, before Eve was a twinkle in Adam's eye. A vow simply means that you seriously promise to do or not do a specific thing. Whatever that "thing" is, you are adamant about keeping and making an agreement to do or not do it. So to whom did you make your vows? You thought you made them to your husband, right? No! According to the scriptures we just discussed, when you entered the constitution of marriage, you were making a commitment to God, to take care of his son, your husband, and to be his help meet…his wife. Do you know how God feels about vows?

> *When thou vowest a vow unto God, defer not to pay it; for he hath no pleasure in fools: pay that which thou hast vowed. Better is it that thou shouldest not vow, than that thou shouldest vow and not pay. Suffer not thy mouth to cause thy flesh to sin; neither say thou before the angel, that it was an error: wherefore should God be angry at thy voice, and destroy the work of thine hands? (Ecclesiastes 5:4-6)*

As far as the Lord is concerned, if you are not going to keep the vow you made unto Him, don't even make the vow. God said don't allow (or suffer) your mouth to get you in trouble with Him. Or to say I made a mistake; it was an error. You need to be sure and if you're unsure, it's best not to enter the marriage with uncertainty, only hurting yourself and possibly children.

When you are not committed to keeping your vows, you tie God's hands from allowing favor to reign in your marriage.

How silly is it to go into a marriage thinking it won't last? What did you get married for? Why put yourself through so much emotional stress?

If a man desires to marry you, ask the Lord if it's His will. Honey, listen: you are God's daughter and He gets VERY UPSET when people mistreat His children. He's merciful, forgiving and gracious, waiting to see if that person will come to His senses, but wives…when God gets angry, tell me who will stop Him? He's God. He made everything!!! Therefore, if you have ANY reservations, don't do it! Wait until you're sure.

If you are certain, why not talk to the Lord and ask him to bless your union and that He (God) remains in the forefront? Since you are committed to living for Him, I'm sure you have a relationship with God and you consult him on everything so He can direct you right? Just because the Lord grants you the desires of your heart that does not mean that your relationship with Him diminishes. If anything it should become stronger with you AND your husband acknowledging Him about everything.

> *In all thy ways acknowledge him, and he shall direct thy paths. (Proverbs 3:6)*

Remember love is unselfish. When you truly love someone, you care about their well-being and you want what is best for them. So wives, let's look at the traditional vows again.

For Better or For Worse

- Will you still be willing to "hang in there" if the two of you learned that your husband found out he had a child from a one-night stand before meeting you?

- What if one of his grandparents fell ill and needed to move in with you for support and care. Would you sacrifice your happily ever after, or ask your husband about someone else in the family taking on the responsibility, or even suggest to your husband a nursing home?
- What if you learned your husband had an irreversible procedure that prevents him from having children? Will you still be committed to the marriage?
- What if your husband's job requires him to be away from home days at a time, leaving you to take care of the house? Can he trust you to be faithful while he is away?

Oftentimes, when we are getting married we don't think about worse; we think about better and happily ever after. What is your marriage built upon? Again, wives, remember Him, the one to whom you made your vows. You made them to the Lord, to take care of His son and Jesus' brother. Jesus said this:

> *Therefore, my beloved brethren, be ye stedfast, unmoveable, always abounding in the work of the Lord, forasmuch as ye know that your labour is not in vain in the Lord. (I Corinthians 15:58)*

Being a wife is labor and it takes effort to make it work. Know that your work for the Lord (this labor of love we call marriage) is NOT in vain. If by chance your worse appears, remember we are working for the Lord; Your effort and work you are putting into your commitment are not going unnoticed. STAND STILL! Don't compromise your beliefs and don't waiver in your faith in Jesus. He will always come through. Always remember that there are 3 phases in life: You are in a storm, coming out of a storm or going into a storm. If by chance your husband's faith is wavering, as you both started together in this walk with Christ together, you STILL can have the favor of God in your life if you keep Him first and do His will:

> *For the unbelieving husband is sanctified by the wife, and the unbelieving wife is sanctified by the husband: else were your children unclean; but now are they holy. (I Corinthians 7:14)*

Have you heard the song by Donnie McClurklin that says after you've done all to stand, stand? That means, when you feel like you can't go any further and you feel like you have done everything, when you're weak, that's when you're strong. You're standing because God is holding you up.

> *I waited patiently for the LORD; and he inclined unto me, and heard my cry. He brought me up also out of an horrible pit, out of the miry clay, and set my feet upon a rock, and established my goings. And he hath put a new song in my mouth, even praise unto our God: many shall see it, and fear, and shall trust in the LORD. Blessed is that man that maketh the LORD his trust, and respecteth not the proud, nor such as turn aside to lies. (Psalms 40:1-4)*

For Better or For Worse

- Will you still be willing to commit to your vows if your husband loses his job? Will you become that nagging wife who can't see the effort being made by your husband? Or will you encourage your brother in the Lord (your husband) and you all pray concerning the matter?
- Will you consult the Lord and console your husband through the Word, if you all were told that he had to pay

more in child support from a child born through a previous marriage?
- When you all disagree on a financial matter, does your income always end up being the topic of the conversation, because you make more than he does?
- Will you still commit to your vows you made if you learned your husband's credit score prevents you all from buying the house on the hill with the white picket fence?

Wives, love and marriage are not about the things we possess. Of course, we all want better and I agree that when you get married, you should not be worse off than you were before you got married; but how do you know what you are going through isn't a test of your faith and commitment to God? Surely Job did not foresee all of the sufferings he would encounter and yet he determined that regardless of the outcome, he would hold true to his commitment and integrity in the Lord and whatever the Lord's will would be, it would just have to be that…HIS will.

I can somewhat relate to a testament of faith in my marriage. From day one, my salary was more than my husband's. It never was an issue because I really didn't care nor did it cross my mind until he brought it up as an example and witness to another couple. If we are one, why was it important how much I made? It's more important to ensure that our needs are met and taken care of. When my husband and I got married, there were things I experienced financially that he had not. I experienced going into credit card debt in college and clearing that up to have good credit. I experienced the home-buying process because I had purchased a condo. Because of my experiences, I could share with him what I had gone through and why or why not the loan presented to us for our first home was not good. He honored that, consulted the Lord on OUR behalf and now my husband can make an informed decision based on the information I had given Him and of course with us consulting the Lord FIRST before moving forward with the decision.

> *Submitting yourselves one to another in the fear of God. Wives, submit yourselves unto your own husbands, as unto the Lord. For the husband is the head of the wife, even as Christ is the head of the church: and he is the saviour of the body. (Ephesians 5:21-23)*

How often have we heard this scripture quoted and taken out of context? As a husband and wife, we submit ourselves to each OTHER, fearing God. The fear of God meaning, we don't want to do anything to frustrate the grace of God in our lives and in our marriage. We fear that God means what He says and if we go against His will, we make ourselves vulnerable and open ourselves to sufferings that just could be avoided. Yes, God made the husband head of the wife, which means that husband is the covering, because of Eve's disobedience. There is divine order in everything God does. There's the husband, the wife, children and then the dog (if you have a pet). As the head, the husband is the provider and covering. He is the umbrella, as long as He is following Christ. When that man is not following Christ, there are holes in that umbrella and oftentimes a marriage can suffer things unnecessarily because the covering isn't lining up. But honey, if you are a praying wife and you have committed your life to the Lord, to do a service well pleasing to Him, you can go over that man's head and get an answer for God, on the behalf of your family. The husband being head does not mean: "Woman, you are going to do as I say!" No, we are laborers together and we are the "help meet"; wives help meet the needs.

Continuing with discussion on our test of faith, my husband left his job to assist in the ministry as his grandfather, the Pastor and founder of our church, went through a suffering. There was no hesitation and no argument on my behalf to ask him how we were going to manage. He was doing a work for the Lord. Why would I fear? The Lord is the provider and had been providing thus far.

Surely, God wouldn't bring us this far to leave us. So what did I do? We just said, okay Lord, we are following you. It was weird (and we've often reflected on this scenario and discussed it) because there was no doubt, no thoughts of "what if," and no fear at all.

Before my husband proceeded with leaving his job, I prayed because I had established a relationship with the Lord first, before I met my husband. I was a wife to the Lord, so HE KNEW who I was. I said Lord, I thank you that you found us faithful to put my husband in this position (he was already a minister; he left his job as a police officer and became Assistant Pastor) and I thank you that you will meet our needs. Guess what? He did. Wives listen. We can't please God without faith and if you don't have faith, it's sin.

> *But without faith it is impossible to please him: for he that cometh to God must believe that he is, and that he is a rewarder of them that diligently seek him. (Hebrews 11:6)*

Impossible means it CANNOT be done. If you don't believe in God, you cannot please Him and you surely can't get the desires of your heart.

> *...for whatsoever is not of faith is sin. (Romans 14:23)*

Really, God is saying, it's either all or nothing at all; either you believe me or you don't and if you don't then its sin. God told us something else. He said He is not like us.

> *God is not a man, that he should lie; neither the son of man, that he should repent: hath he said, and shall he not do it? or hath he spoken, and shall he not make it good? (Numbers 23:19)*

Honey, if He said He would do it, then He's going to do it! So I was crazy enough to believe Jesus because He has proven himself every time. Hey, thank God, wives, that He allowed you to get an education and a degree to have a career – but your career means nothing with God. What's more important is standing on the principles of God. God forbid you have a child and you have to take an extended absence because of a difficult pregnancy. God said this in His word about riches:

> *A GOOD name is rather to be chosen than great riches, and loving favour rather than silver and gold. (Proverbs 22:1)*

In the world, when you seek to purchase a house, car or apply for a job or credit card, you are known by your credit score. We are judged by our credit score. It tells a creditor if you pay your bills on time, if you're consistent, if you have stability (jobs perform credit checks as well). Wives, when you say you are representing the Lord you have to stand for the truth and pay your bills that you created. Jesus also said this:

> *Owe no man anything, but to love one another: for he that loveth another hath fulfilled the law. (Romans 13:8)*

Wives, are we really representing the Lord if we can't pay our bills on time or have to buy something new for every church service or every event? Or you can't get those Coach shoes or Gucci purse? It's okay to enjoy things of value but make sure you can afford them. Don't compromise paying a bill for an item of clothing. Take care of your necessities first! Don't be silly!

In Sickness and In Health

- Will you treat that husband the same, if he had an accident occur on the job where he hurt his back and he became dependent upon your help…help meet?
- What if your husband were in an accident that paralyzed him from the waist down and he was unable to provide the "milk" to your "cookies" (keeping this G-rated), preventing you all from having children, will you still be in love?
- What if your husband became suddenly blind and could no longer compliment you, and he could only see life through your eyes? Would the life he would now experience become cold, lonely and heartless or heartfelt, breathtaking and peaceful?

These are just examples of what we don't expect to occur in our marriage but they could occur as a testament to our will, commitment, faith to our Savior Jesus Christ, and our spouse. Being married and being a wife is a service; it's a ministry, a vow to the Lord that everything you do, you do to Him, the Lord Jesus.

And whatsoever ye do, do it heartily, as to the Lord, and not unto men; (Colossians 3:23)

Remember, if Jesus Christ is the head of your life and you are pleasing Him, you will automatically please your husband because you are living according to the principles of God. Wives, if you and your husband commit to this vow, then any other vows can be built upon this:

> *And if it seems evil to you to serve the LORD, choose for yourselves this day that you will serve, whether the gods which your fathers served that were on the other side of the River, or the gods of the Amorites, in whose land you dwell. But as for me and my house, we will serve the LORD." (Joshua 24:15)*

Whom will you serve in your house? Let's say you accepted Jesus as your personal savior during your marriage (your husband had not). Everything started off well as you paid your tithes, studied the word, and attended church services. You didn't have an abundance of money left over after bills were paid, but somehow your needs were met and your family had lack of nothing. In fact, the Lord often told you to be a blessing to specific people in your life and made a way for you to do so. All of a sudden, it seemed as if nothing was working out as you supposed it should or the way you were used to things coming together. Something changed. As you consulted the Lord and asks for guidance, you got weary in your well doing. You became impatient with the Lord, so you decided that being "saved" isn't the life for you and "you were going to do you." You ranted, cried out, even spoke to God as if He were like you and I, getting an attitude with Him; yet and still, the situation did not change. Do you know why it didn't work? You became impatient and did not CONTINUE in the Lord:

> *And let us not be weary in well doing: for in due season we shall reap, if we faint not. (Galatians 6:9)*

Then, you became dependent upon you versus the Lord and you came to the Lord as a last resort when things didn't go your way. Jesus said:

> *I am Alpha and Omega, the beginning and the end, the first and the last. (Revelation 22:13)*

Jesus WILL NOT take a back seat to no one or nothing. So after you're ranting and shouting and saying God is not good to you because He didn't help you, think about your situation. Did you consult the Lord FIRST? Did you come to him FIRST or did you try your own solution and THEN come running to Jesus when it failed?

Don't get me wrong. Jesus is concerned about us and wants to help us, but He doesn't want to be used for a short term fix. He wants to be an integral part of your life. "Doing you" is what got you in the mess you were in. God isn't moved by your sob story and sad face or your decision to stop coming to church and go back to death because something didn't happen in YOUR time frame. God moves by your faith:

> *Now faith is the substance of things hoped for, the evidence of things not seen. (Hebrews 11:1)*

Now means present...currently happening. The faith you have works for you NOW and is the substance (or the basis... primary source) of whatever it is you desire (or hope for) to have. That faith is also the primary, fundamental element of what you don't see. If you see it or have it, why would you want it? You already have it. What sense would it made to want to have a family gathering for Thanksgiving (which you already had) and it's Christmas? What do your vows mean to you? Were they just words spoken for the event or did you carefully consider the actions to be taken behind them?

Things to Consider

What is preventing you from totally submitting to the vows made? Are there people in your life that you need to separate yourself from to come back to your "first love"? Are there circumstances that have caused you to forget what your vows mean to the Lord and to your marriage?

Virtuous Assessment

Review the commitment (vow) you made with Christ and your husband. Don't be concerned with what your spouse is/is not doing. This is about YOUR walk with Christ and YOUR commitment to take care of His son (your husband). The Bible says that although you become one when you wed, we as individuals will be accountable for what we do. So evaluate your commitment and what you have been doing.

1. Have you kept the vows that you have made?

2. Write a list of areas in which you can improve on.

3. If that list uncovers some blemishes, ask the Lord and your husband for forgiveness for not upholding your vows. Things just may be going well, but have you really totally given your all or just enough to get by?

4. Place that list in your favorite scripture in the Bible and leave it there.

5. Challenge yourself for three months and at the end of the three months go back and review the list to determine if you have recommitted wholeheartedly to your vows.

Chapter 7

How to Be a Wife

To be a wife you must first understand who you are in the Lord and how important you are to the Lord and to your husband. God says:

He who finds a wife finds a good thing, And obtains favor from the LORD (Proverbs 18:22)

He who finds a wife… means you're first being a wife unto the Lord. Next, the verse says once the man of God finds a wife he found a good thing! Wives, God called us good. Everything He made was good and VERY good. Lastly, when that man finds that woman being a wife until the Lord and that man gets his "good thing," he gets his favor from the Lord. The Lord will be EXCEPTIONALLY KIND unto that man because He has found a wife (who honors the Lord FIRST), who is unwilling to compromise her beliefs and what she stands for in Christ Jesus! Wives, our men need our love, support, attention, encouragement, dedication, commitment (to the Lord first and to him), guidance, respect, knowledge, presence…everything. If the Lord felt man could do it alone, why would he say it wasn't good for Adam to be alone and God would make the man some help? Being a wife is a process as you learn each other's habits, likes and dislikes. Learning how to be a wife will be new but should become natural because you were already being a wife unto the Lord and taking care of your own business. Now you are responsible for helping take care of someone else's business which impacts you! There's no "this is mine." It's ours in a relationship. Jesus said:

> *And said, for this cause shall a man leave father and mother, and shall cleave to his wife: and they twain shall be one flesh? Wherefore they are no more twain, but one flesh. What therefore God hath joined together, let not man put asunder. (Matthew 19:5-6)*

When you get married, you are one flesh; not one spirit. While we are one together, yet we serve one God and we have one Spirit (God's Spirit) dwelling in us but we all must give an account of what we do as individuals. So yours becomes ours! If you wanted to be by yourself wives, you probably should have stayed by yourself. I'm sorry but that's the harsh reality. Again, the question is what were your intentions for marriage and what were your expectations? There are many aspects to being a wife. Let's take a look at some of them.

Virtuous Assessment

The definition of a guide is to assist (a person); to provide direction. A guide is someone who serves as a model for others. So if we are guides, we are assisting our husbands and providing direction to our children, of whom we are also role models. As stated earlier, the man (husband) is the covering, the provider, the strength, the leader; but a woman of God...OH MY GOD...has the power to drive success or defeat...the power to bring peace to a house, or evil. We serve as a model, meaning the children and husband look to us, by way of Jesus Christ, for direction and leadership in the house. If that's not a huge responsibility then I'm confused. No need to worry wives; look at the ultimate example of a guide that we have:

> *Howbeit when he, the Spirit of truth, is come, he will guide you into all truth: for he shall not speak of himself; but whatsoever he shall hear, that shall he speak: and he will shew you things to come. (John 16:13)*

The Holy Spirit (the Spirit of Truth) will guide us into all truths. He is not selfish; he doesn't even talk about himself. He speaks the Word of God and shows us things to come so there are no surprises. Wives, shouldn't we be truthful when we are guiding the house and managing finances (if you and your husband have agreed that you are better with handling finances)? What's done in the dark comes to the light. If you're scheming to get more money so you can fulfill your own selfish pleasures, please don't think that it will not come up and that spouse will not find out…because he will, especially if that spouse is a man of God and doing his service well pleasing to the Lord.

Chapter 8

Parenting

One of the most beautiful, indescribable experiences in life is to give birth to life. What unexplainable joy it is to experience feel something moving on the inside, watching your abdomen stretch and take form, occasionally seeing an indentation of a hand or a foot stretch forward or to move when you or your husband speak or read! Childbearing brings forth patience as you finally see the face, feet and hands that have been punching you for so long and you soon realize that it was all worth it! Wives, God told us to guide the house and raise children unto Him. We have discussed in the single ladies section of this book how children have all of our features and characteristics but they do not belong to us; but we are also accountable for teaching these children the principles and standards of God.

> *...but bring them up in the nurture and admonition of the Lord. (Ephesians 6:4)*

We are held accountable for our children until they grow up and have the ability to make their own decisions. As they grow and become adults, the decisions made should be based upon the small seeds planted in their lives by us, on a daily basis on how to live responsibly and be accountable for their actions.

Train up a child in the way he should go, and when he is old he will not depart from it. (Proverbs 22:6)

How Do You Train a Child?

Training means you are directing or instructing someone. Imagine you being a trainer, teaching others how to use Microsoft Word, which is a word-processing software that's typically used for typing documents on a computer. This means you will have had to experience all of the various scenarios, uses, shortcuts, etc., to educate someone else. If you have not experienced every scenario and don't know all the answers, you have other resources accessible to obtain the answers. So it is with raising a child. Although you may not know the answers, you have a guide, a road map on what to do, to be successful. Wives, we have the wisdom of older women such as our parents, grandparents and mentors. We also have the Word of God. To train a child:

1. We have to be an example of patience, commitment and how you live, love and have faith:

> *Let no man despise thy youth; but be thou an example of the believers, in word, in conversation, in charity, in spirit, in faith, in purity. (I Timothy 4:12)*

2. We have to live wholeheartedly for the Lord and his Spirit has to dwell in us to teach our children the principles of God and to walk how Jesus walks:

> *If we live in the Spirit, let us also walk in the Spirit. (Galatians 5:25)*

3. Wives we must lead by example. To give love, peace, patience, temperance, we must demonstrate that, which can only come through the Spirit of the living God:

> *But the fruit of the Spirit is love, joy, peace, longsuffering, gentleness, goodness, faith, Meekness, temperance: against such there is no law. (Galatians 5:22-23)*

4. A guide teaches how to never give up on goals and aspirations, regardless of what others may feel or say to discourage you.

> *I can do all things through Christ which strengtheneth me. (Philippians 4:13)*

5. A guide teaches how to always seek God's guidance and approval before setting out to do anything.

> *In all thy ways acknowledge him, and he shall direct thy paths. (Proverbs 3:6)*

> *Seek ye the LORD while he may be found, call ye upon him while he is near. (Isaiah 55:6)*

6. We must teach our children to be responsible.

> *Therefore all things whatsoever ye would that men should do to you, do ye even so to them: (Matthew 7:12)*

7. Wives, we MUST teach our children to tell the truth, regardless of the outcome.

> *The lip of truth shall be established for ever: but a lying tongue is but for a moment. (Proverbs 12:19)*

> *Blessed is that man that maketh the LORD his trust, and respecteth not the proud, nor such as turn aside to lies (Psalms 40:4)*

8. Wives, we must teach our children the value of life versus the value of money and if they seek wisdom and knowledge, they will experience the blessings that come from God.

> *But seek ye first the kingdom of God, and his righteousness; and all these things shall be added unto you. (Matthew 6:33)*

9. As a guide, wives, our children must know they have to be respectful of their parents and others.

> *Children, obey your parents in the Lord: for this is right. Honour thy father and mother; which is the first commandment with promise; That it may be well with thee, and thou mayest live long on the earth. (Ephesians 6:1-3)*

10. Wives, we have to teach our children to learn how to not be revengeful and trust that the Lord, the heavyweight champion of all time, will come through on their behalf:

> *But I say unto you, Love your enemies, bless them that curse you, do good to them that hate you, and pray for them which despitefully use you, and persecute you; That ye may be the children of your Father which is in heaven: for he maketh his sun to rise on the evil and on the good, and sendeth rain on the just and on the unjust. (Matthew 5:44-45)*

> *The LORD shall fight for you, and ye shall hold your peace. (Exodus 14:14)*

11. Finally, wives, our children must know how important they are to us and to the Lord.

> *Lo, children are an heritage of the LORD: and the fruit of the womb is his reward. (Psalms 127:3)*

> *And they brought young children to him, that he should touch them: and his disciples rebuked those that brought them. But when Jesus saw it, he was much displeased, and said unto them, Suffer the little children to come unto me, and forbid them not: for of such is the kingdom of God. (Mark 10:13-14)*

When the disciples reprimanded those who wanted Jesus to touch their children, Jesus got upset and said allow the children to come to me! I cannot express the importance of knowing that children do NOT belong to us. They belong to the Lord. He requires and depends on us wives to not only be examples to the children but also to teach them the ways of Christ. The blessings of God are passed on from generation to generation but how can they be passed on if the generations don't know WHO the blessor is, WHAT the blessing(s) are and WHY and HOW they are obtained? As Jesus stated, wives, we MUST be about our Father's business!

Chapter 9

Discretion

Oh Lord! Here we go. Wives, we often become so absorbed with our family lives and commitments that we need a break from it all. So we meet up with women that we keep in contact with via email, Facebook and Twitter. These are women whom we have had lasting relationships with: old high school friends, college acquaintances, current co-workers, family members who are also dear friends, sisters in Christ… the list continues on. Just as we have and need outlets, so do our spouses; but for some reason, our outlets turn into "sessions" that become male bashing. Wives, let's think about this. When you took your vows for better or for worse, remember the two of you became one. So when you are speaking ill of your husband, you are speaking ill of yourself. If you don't like the "atmosphere" you have the power to change it. In other words, if there's something not going right in your marriage, according to the principles of God, you can do something about it. Someone has to represent Jesus and we must learn discretion.

Being discreet means that you are showing good judgment or discernment in how you behave. It's not only having wisdom but also using wisdom in a situation. Let's use the example above again in more detail. You have five female acquaintances whom you call close friends that you've been with and shared personal details, triumphs, fears and defeats with. You all have been congregating for ten years. Two are married and three are not. You all meet and play catch up on what's going in your lives over dinner. Some mentioning major events such as engagements, moves, expecting children or just things going on, on the job and with other co-workers as well as mutual acquaintances you all may know. How easy would it be to begin complaining about things going on in your marriage?

Let me ask you this. What good would it do? Although these are women that you trust and confide in but if they don't have the mind of Christ, you're just making a lot of noise and saying nothing. To continue with the example, let's say you do begin to complain about financial woes you're having and how you handle money as opposed to your spouse or how he works long hours and doesn't spend time with you (always having something else to do); or he is just overly exhausted when he comes home, insomuch as to not hold a meaningful conversation when he arrives home from work.

Honey…listen! While you may trust these women, oftentimes they know someone that knows someone that knows the two of you. Once again Satan is eagerly waiting to devour you. Please don't think that this news won't travel and cause a rift in your marriage. Almost always…somehow an email, text, word of mouth…something comes up and your spouse will find out. There's a woman somewhere, who once had a high school crush on your husband and just by chance knows one of your friends or is related to one of your five acquaintances. They are just having idle conversation about those friends and learn that you are married to her high school sweetheart. Hmph!! She will somehow run into your husband and she gone put her best foot forward. She will have on her best attire, hair and nails fixed and appear to have it all together but believe me – and of course we know it's a set up. Whose fault is it? Surely you don't think it's yours right?

Think again. Listen:

> *Wherein in time past ye walked according to the course of this world, according to the prince of the power of the air, the spirit that now worketh in the children of disobedience (Ephesians 2:2)*

According to this scripture, the same spirit that works in disobedient children (surely we know disobedience is not of God) is the prince of the power of the air. That means news travels, honey, and you put it out there. Where does your help come from? Our help comes from the Lord almighty, which made heaven and earth. If He is our help, why don't we consult Him FOR help? If He is ruler over our lives, why don't we let Him rule? I'm in no way saying that if you're going through you have to get through on your own or can't confide in someone, but make sure the people you're confiding in can help you! Confide in someone you know that can get a prayer through! Don't seek for someone who will side with your story, seek for wisdom. Misery loves company as we have heard countless times throughout our lives, so why consult with someone who is in a bad situation? Unless you and your friends are seeking for God's wisdom in your situations, looking to His word for direction and in prayer on each other's behalf, you will more than likely leave the gathering feeling more hurt and angry at your husband about the situation than allowing the peace of God to rest in your lives.

Here another issue with discretion. We are a society that when someone asks how we are doing, we are ready to explode; we tell EVERYTHING! We feel as if we have to explain ourselves or explain an event that has occurred in our lives. Listen, if you aren't in a position to help me, to encourage or uplift me, SURELY I'm not going to pour out my life journal to you so you can make my life an open book to others. In fact, Jesus said:

> *When wisdom entereth into thine heart, and knowledge is pleasant unto thy soul; Discretion shall preserve thee, understanding shall keep thee (Proverbs 2:10-11)*

Here's another example. We also find that when situations arise, we run to our family. We begin talking about that man (he's THAT man now, not our husband) and everything he has not done, only telling our side. Honey, there are three sides (not two) to every story: your side, my side and God's side. So you are pouring your heart out and your family is pissed off to the highest point of pisstivity (can I say this? Well, I just have to be me. Wives, you all should know me a little better by reading this book that I am just me…shoot)!

Now, you have all the ammunition you need to go home and continue your cold-shoulder approach. What your family don't know is that you and your husband sought marital counseling through your Pastor, have realized and accepted where you BOTH were wrong and are now back on the right path. Meanwhile, when he comes around, your family is still holding a grudge and planting negative seeds about him, suggesting you leave. Wives, wives, wives! I have heard countless times that when you married that husband, you are marrying his family.

Honey…if I had to marry my husband's family, I would NOT have married him and I'm certain my husband feels the same. Your family won't provide for you or clean when you're feeling ill. Your family may take the kids every now and then but ummm…they won't be staying the night. Hmph, CHILEPLEASE!!!! They will be returned THAT DAY! Why would Jesus say that a man should LEAVE his father and mother and cleave or stick with his wife and the two of them should be one? Stop trying to prove your point and prove God's point!

If you're in a discussion with your spouse and you feel the discussion can cause either of you to have an attitude, don't respond. I'm not saying to be disrespectful but what I am saying is one person can't argue alone. It takes two. Leave the room in a non-threatening manner. Well, we ARE speaking of living according to the principles of the Lord, right? So Jesus said do this:

> *If it be possible, as much as lieth in you, live peaceably with all men. (Romans 12:18)*

Jesus said as much as is in YOU…YOU live in peace with all men! Don't worry about what someone else is or isn't doing, YOU represent Christ. Well, if you say you have the Spirit of God living within you, then you have ALL THAT YOU NEED INSIDE OF YOU to do according to the word of God. That may mean, getting the Bible and reading scriptures to remind you of who you represent or to ask yourself, if this were Jesus you were speaking to how would you talk to Him? Would you disrespect Him? At the end of the day, we don't know what tomorrow will bring. We don't know what lies ahead. Therefore, it's important not to go to bed angry. Don't give Satan any room in your house. Don't let him stay anywhere!

> *Be ye angry, and sin not: let not the sun go down upon your wrath: Neither give place to the devil. (Ephesians 4:26-27)*

Your bedroom should be a place of peace and comfort. Even if it's "pillow talk" time, time to laugh or reflect on things that have happened during the day, it shouldn't be a place where the last thing you're thinking about or discussing is a negative situation that occurred with your husband. God says He gives us "sweet" sleep:

> *When thou liest down, thou shalt not be afraid: yea, thou shalt lie down, and thy sleep shall be sweet. (Proverbs 3:24)*

Discretion doesn't have to have a negative connotation. We often associate it with not sharing with others when things go wrong in our marriage. Oftentimes, it may be that we may need to be mum on some blessings that are coming our way. I'm sure you have heard: "Don't let your left hand know what your right hand is doing?" Listen, in case you haven't realized it by now, God is infinite in wisdom and the wisdom and knowledge we have, He gave to us. You don't think He knows?

> *...he that teacheth man knowledge, shall not he know? (Psalms 94:10)*

He often plants a vision or a seed to move forward with a business or a not-for-profit organization or to discreetly help someone in need (who we may feel in our minds, from outward appearance, don't need the help).

> *And the LORD answered me, and said, write the vision, and make it plain upon tables, that he may run that readeth it. For the vision is yet for an appointed time, but at the end it shall speak, and not lie: though it tarry, wait for it; because it will surely come, it will not tarry. (Habakkuk 2:2-3)*

Since we know God has all knowledge, it is He that gave you the vision!! That's why it is imperative to acknowledge the Lord on how to move forward with whatever vision He has given you. Here's the catch...honey, when you think that close friend or family member would be excited, they come out of another bag. Instead of saying that's awesome, let's touch and agree because God said if two or three of us touch and agree on anything He would do it:

> *Again I say unto you, that if two of you shall agree on earth as touching anything that they shall ask, it shall be done for them of my Father which is in heaven. (Matthew 18:19)*

So we agree that he will lead you in a plain path…but "they" are telling you why they don't think you should do what you have a desire to do and what YOUR current situation looks like. Meanwhile on the inside you wanna say: "You don't know my situation." Maybe they do; because you told them your financial situation. Wives, one thing I learned about Jesus is…He doesn't need money.

> *Ho, every one that thirsteth, come ye to the waters, and he that hath no money; come ye, buy, and eat; yea, come, buy wine and milk without money and without price. (Isaiah 55:1)*

He SPEAKS! When HE SPEAKS!!!!!! OH JESUS!!! Things happen. God spoke the world into existence, He spoke conception in Mary (Jesus's mother) AND Elizabeth (her cousin), He spoke and told Lazarus to come out of the grave, He spoke peace in your life, He told death to move…it wasn't your time yet!!! Wives, wives, wives…LISTEN!!!! Then, Jesus had the NERVE.. the audacity to say…BEHOLD…give unto YOU that same power…wait wait wait; then he said greater works than what I did on this earth, you can do, because I AM IN YOU!!! You betta shut the front door and slam the back one. Don't believe me? Hmph:

But you shall receive power when the Holy Spirit has come upon you…(Acts 1:8)

Verily, verily, I say unto you, He that believeth on me, the works that I do shall he do also; and greater works than these shall he do; because I go unto my Father. And whatsoever ye shall ask in my name, that will I do, that the Father may be glorified in the Son. (John 14:12-13)

We having the same spirit of faith, according as it is written, I believed, and therefore have I spoken; we also believe, and therefore speak; (2 Corinthians 4:13)

Stop speaking defeat and speak victory! Jesus believed what He spoke because He knew WHO He represented and what He (God) was capable of! Speak peace and not evil, speak life into your marriage and not death, speak success and not failure in your children, speak encouragement and not discouragement, speak love and not hatred.

Discretion will keep you safe, maintain you, and protect you. Discretion only comes when you get wisdom and knowledge. It's a learned behavior that was either instilled or you learned by experience. We learn to be discreet in our affairs and as wives to our husbands and to the Lord. It's important that we learn how to be discreet, when to act, when to speak so that when we do, it is with so much power and authority, we COMMAND the room! THAT'S the power of a praying wife and God-fearing woman!

Chapter 10

Love, as God Loves

There's not enough emphasis that can be placed on love. In fact, love is the center of it all, whether you are single or married.

Wives, the man you married…is this man you say you love? Here is the conclusion of love. Either you sincerely love your spouse or you don't and if you don't have the love of God to share with your spouse and to all, all is not lost. You can obtain it. Here is the purest definition of love:

> *Though I speak with the tongues of men and of angels, but have not love, I have become sounding brass or a clanging cymbal. And though I have the gift of prophecy, and understand all mysteries and all knowledge, and though I have all faith, so that I could remove mountains, but have not love, I am nothing. And though I bestow all my goods to feed the poor, and though I give my body to be burned, [a] but have not love, it profits me nothing. Love suffers long and is kind; love does not envy; love does not parade itself, is not puffed up; does not behave rudely, does not seek its own, is not provoked, thinks no evil; does not rejoice in iniquity, but rejoices in the truth; bears all things, believes all things, hopes all things, endures all things; And now*

abide faith, hope, love, these three; but the greatest of these is love. (I Corinthians 13:1-7, 13)

Things to Consider

Wives, I understand that there are various circumstances where it's easy to conclude that you have been doing your part as a wife. The discussion on husbands is another one in and of itself; but we are talking about us wives doing a service unto the Lord. Not to man! A commitment and vow we made unto the Lord to take care of His son. So don't worry about what someone else is or is not doing. You do your part. One thing God does not like is for someone to take advantage of his child and He said He will fight for you if you only let Him. Just hold your peace. So, as we seek to become better wives let us consider this. When our husbands leave the house to go to work, to the store, or take our children to school, should someone see them out, who is that husband representing? He's representing the family! He's a reflection of the entire household.

Wives, when we are out with our husbands, let's say at a work event and we are introduced to co-workers and supervisors, who are we representing? We are representing that husband. Most will look to that wife to see her expression and mannerisms. Based on her body language, folks will make an informed decision about how well your marriage is doing and if you're happy. Wives, our children are a reflection of us! Based on their conduct and appearance at school, the mother will be blamed or praised. If your children's coats are filthy, shoes dirty, with no hats or gloves during the cold months, people are going to look to that wife. Why? Again, we guide the house. We have a huge responsibility. Most times, if everything is going well in a marriage, the wife is praised (think about it). Let's bring this full circle. When we say that Jesus Christ is our Lord and Savior, we are representing Him. Everywhere we go, in everything we do, what we say and who we say it to, how we raise our children and treat our spouse, how we love unconditionally, our relationship with the Lord, praying always on the behalf of our family and the body of Christ! Based on your conduct today, would Jesus deny you as his representation? Would He say: "Uh uh, she's not representing me? I don't know her; the thoughts she has and the behavior she's displaying are not of me." Or would He say: "Yes, we have the same Spirit; I know her! That's MY sister. I am in her and she is in me!"

> *Put on therefore, as the elect of God, holy and beloved, bowels of mercies, kindness, humbleness of mind, meekness, longsuffering; Forbearing one another, and forgiving one another, if any man have a quarrel against any: even as Christ forgave you, so also do ye. And above all these things put on charity, which is the bond of perfectness. And let the peace of God rule in your hearts, to the which also ye are called in one body; and be ye thankful. Let the word of Christ dwell in you richly in all wisdom; teaching and admonishing one another in psalms and hymns and spiritual songs, singing with grace in your hearts to the Lord. And whatsoever ye do in word or deed, do all in the name of the Lord Jesus, giving thanks to God and the Father by him. Wives, submit yourselves unto your own husbands, as it is fit in the Lord. Husbands, love your wives, and be not bitter against them. (Colossians 3:12-19)*

Virtuous Assessment

1. Wives, consider your ways. Whom have you been trying to please? Yourself? Your husband? If you have been trying to please your husband, write down how or what you have been doing to try to please your husband.

2. Take that same list you made about what you have been doing to please your husband and seek to please the Lord. When you please the Lord and do His will, you'll please your husband.

   When a man's ways please the LORD, he maketh even his enemies to be at peace with him. (Proverbs 16:7)

3. If you're representing Christ, have you been teaching your children about your savior? Take a half hour before their bed time to teach them about the Bible. Show them the table of contents, how to find books in the Bible, how many books there are. As they get older, explain what the little numbers and letters next to specific words in a verse mean; show them how to study. There's a website called www.OrientalTrading.com. When you search there on "fun" and "faith," you'll find all kinds of bible study material for children that help make learning fun. Take time with them. We all lead busy, hectic lives but your love and attention is what they crave and desire as they seek your approval. Take the time to compliment them on projects and accomplishments. Encourage them when they go astray to assure them that your love and God's love for them is unconditional and doesn't change. Pray as a family.

4. Where did the fun go? When did your marriage become such a hassle? When did you stop "liking" each other and not enjoying one another's company? Try to identify where and when things begin to change. If that means seeking marriage counseling, then consult the Lord first and ask Him to lead you on how to approach your husband (most men do not welcome the idea of another

"man," whether that be a Pastor or not, telling them how to run their household, not recognizing it is the Spirit of God in that Pastor that is assisting). By consulting the Lord and praying together first, this trap can be avoided.

Chapter 11

The Sacrifice

Simply stated, marriage is a sacrifice. As a child, you may have been brought up to clean the bathtub as soon as you get out, regardless if you showered or took a bath. Or you may have been taught to only use your face towel once and to wash the towels in the evening so that the wet towels don't sour and smell overnight. Wives, you may have been taught to spank your children if they do something that goes against the morals and values you're instilling. On the other hand, your husband may have been taught to hang up that face towel to air dry and use it in the morning before leaving for the day and then wash those towels in the morning, or have that child stand and face the wall as a time out for not-so-good behavior. The point being made is now as you become one, your lives become intertwined and you determine what will be best for you and your household. There are so many sacrifices in marriage. What I have learned to be the biggest challenge for some (not all wives) is intimacy. The husband wants to be intimate on a regular basis. His definition and your definition of regular are totally different. Wives, our definition of "regular" is contingent upon these criteria:

- How stressful our day was at work.
- How much housework we have to do when we get home

because we left before our husband and when we returned he MUST have been rushing because his socks are on the floor, dishes are in the sink and there are food stains on the table where he and the children ate.
- If there are children how much homework they have and what extracurricular activities they may have that evening.
- If we have to prepare dinner.

Based on these criteria, wives, the mood has been already set...NO MILK AND COOKIES because we are in defense mode. In fact, we left a text or sent an email as soon as we got home from work because he is just not making it easier. It seems like everything is on us, Right? So "regular" for us MAY be once a week, when the children are asleep and chileplease, don't wake me up when I'm in a "coma-like" sleep and I have to get up at 5 a.m. to go to work!!! Hubby's time is between 11 p.m. and 1 a.m. Sounds about right? Well...wives....you know we have to see what Jesus said:

> *Now concerning the things of which you wrote to me: It is good for a man not to touch a woman. Nevertheless, because of sexual immorality, let each man have his own wife, and let each woman have her own husband. Let the husband render to his wife the affection due her, and likewise also the wife to her husband. The wife does not have authority over her own body, but the husband does. And likewise the husband does not have authority over his own body, but the wife does. Do not deprive one another except with consent for a time, that you may give yourselves to fasting and prayer; and come together again so that Satan does not tempt you because of your lack of self-control. (I Corinthians 7:1-5)*

Before you got married, you imagined spending time with this man, sharing intimate moments, cuddling. Now, you can't wait for him to leave out town on business or to work longer shifts (which he is probably intentionally doing anyway, to avoid your rejections). Come on wives; Satan is waiting to disrupt your safe haven…your commitment. Do you really think Satan cares? He's going to use the thing that bothers you the most and the person that's closest to you. While you are complaining and making excuses, Satan is plotting to use that woman on the job, who is always kind to your husband. She smiles and speaks, is very well kept and seems to have it all together. Pleasant on the eye and has a good position in the company. The conversation becomes "co-worker" conversation as they enjoy lunch together with a group of other co-workers, but honey she has a plan (recall just as Jesus needs someone to be used for good, Satan requires someone to be used for evil).

Oh, you didn't know? Nowadays women "say" they prefer a married man because there are no strings attached. She gets what she wants and he can go home to his wife. You know… like grandparents and the relationship with the grandchildren? Ever heard the grandparents say they love their grandchildren and love to spend time but at the end of the day, they love when the children go home to their parents? So now, during your husband's drive home he's thinking of the conversation he had with this younger woman, what she wore, how her hair was combed, the way she looked at him and smiled during lunch, only to come how to his wife who is complaining.

Listen, you both had long days. When you come in from work, would you want to be greeted with complaints? Wives, most men want to feel needed. They want to feel as if they are the most important person in your life. If you have children, they don't want to be pushed in the background. Their thoughts are: "Hey, I was the baby first." When you have more than one child, do you stop loving that first one and give all your love to the baby? Each child has a different need but is equally important to you. Your husband wants to feel that as well. The way a man feels needed is through intimacy. Honey, use your power. I'm not saying that's all you have to do, but if you "scratch" his back…your husband will scratch yours.

God knew that intimacy would be one of the biggest issues men would deal with. Satan knows as well. It's been proven and seen in many scenarios in the Bible. But Jesus told us not to defraud one another. Defraud means that you are depriving or deprived of something or cheated. Once again, what vows did you make? There's so much to intimacy than the just big BOOM! Watching a movie, reading your word together (after all, didn't you make Jesus the foundation of your relationship?), working out together, cleaning together, cooking together, playing a game as a family (as my seven-year-old daughter would say). These are all private, intimate moments to share with one another. So where did the love go? What is causing so much stress and anger? What is the root of the problem that prevents the two of you from just liking each other?

My husband always says, "Honey, I know you love me but as long as you like me, then we can make it." When you like someone, you enjoy their company. You don't have to go anywhere or do anything; it's just being in that person's presence that makes you smile on the inside. Wives, let's be honest. Do we communicate what our problems are or what the issues are or do we talk to our husband's like they ARE our children? Again, God told us this:

> *Wisdom is the principal thing; therefore get wisdom: and with all thy getting get understanding. (Proverbs 4:7)*

Communication, including understanding and knowing

what you're communicating about, is critical. Most marriages fail or have issues because of the lack of communication or how we communicate to our spouses. If you really take a step back, the issue is really minor. If you both confess Christ, Christ doesn't argue against himself. Who is going to put on Christ and walk as Jesus walks? If you're unequally yoked, then okay, you can understand why you may not be on one accord and you will have to draw your husband through love and kindness; however when you both confess Jesus Christ as your personal Savior, who is going to be the peacemaker?

> *Depart from evil, and do good; seek peace, and pursue it. (Psalms 34:14)*

So who is going to pursue peace in the relationship? Who is going to do well? Think about it this way. If you say God's Spirit (the Holy Spirit) dwells within you, and your husband says He has the Spirit of God as well, who are you arguing with? This is a spiritual walk, right? You're arguing with the Spirit? But wait!!! Jesus said the Spirit doesn't fight against itself.

> *And if a house be divided against itself, that house cannot stand. (Mark 3:25)*

If you're warring against each other, your marriage will not stand. It won't work.

Can two walk together, except they be agreed? (Amos 3:3)

I would never impose my beliefs on anyone but I will say this: God gives us a choice to decide whom we will live for. Again, as stated before, God said that we should choose who we will serve. Whether you accept it or not, you will be serving someone or something…evil or good. Look at it from this perspective. Imagine that in working on a project, you become acquainted with someone you have never worked with. As you all develop a work relationship, because of this project, you become close acquaintances, having lunch on occasion, talking about various problems or issues you are experiencing, difficulties in relationships and maybe even some health concerns you or close relatives may be going through. You soon learn that this person has taken the information you have shared with them to destroy you and your career. As soon as you found out it was this acquaintance you trusted, who has been sewing discord and planting negative seeds about you, you would in no doubt distance yourself and leave that person alone. Well, that's what Satan does. Listen wives, we don't know Satan at all, but he wants to DEVOUR you.

> *Be sober, be vigilant; because your adversary the devil, as a roaring lion, walketh about, seeking whom he may devour (I Peter 5:8)*

Devour means to completely destroy you…to consume you and yet YOU don't know who Satan REALLY is. You never met him but you befriended him by doing the things that he likes because he sent an illusion that these things were pleasurable. He lures you in to think that doing things that go against the Word of God are fun and enjoyable and living for Christ is boring. No doubt some of the things we did do, when we didn't live for Christ, we enjoyed – but the pleasure ended in hurt and there was never any peace. On the other hand, you also have someone you had not met before, which is Jesus Christ and He only promised peace, joy and love even in situations that look dim. Look at the conversation God had with Satan:

> *Again there was a day when the sons of God came to present themselves before the LORD, and Satan came also among them to present himself before the LORD. And the LORD said unto Satan, From whence comest thou? And Satan answered the LORD, and said, From going to and fro in the earth, and from walking up and down in it (Job 2:1-2)*

So God was having a conversation with His sons and Satan came amongst them as well. God said (I'm paraphrasing): "Hey, where you coming from?" Satan says: "Oh, just going back forth, walking around." I Peter also says Satan is walking around seeing just who he can utterly consume…in pieces. Listen, he wants to destroy you for none other than selfish reasons because he ruined his opportunity and cannot have an eternal life that consists of peace, joy and love; so he wants to destroy and deny your promises and yet you continue to choose to follow him? Just like the example of the co-worker who set you up, Satan is setting you up for failure and you are falling for it! Think about how you so desired for your (at that time) soon-to-be husband to hold you, kiss you and be with you. The scent of his cologne made you smile. His breath was always pleasant and his style was in a class of its own. Now, all of a sudden, you can't stand for him to touch you; his breath doesn't smell but it just smells like BREATH so you don't want him in your face; his kisses are too wet and he wears too much cologne. Really, wives? Don't be silly! Satan is setting you up. God forbid you both choose to separate only to realize that the things you all disagreed about were not worth losing each other. Sacrificing doesn't mean it will always be pleasant. You're giving up something that you enjoy, to see someone else happy. Isn't that what Jesus did? He gave the ultimate sacrifice of his life so that we can experience a life unimaginable with Him in heaven. Why is it so difficult for us to sacrifice a little time for someone we say we love, our husbands?

Things to Consider

Sacrifice means that you are willing to give up something that is of great worth and value to you. What are you willing to sacrifice for your marriage to work? What have you sacrificed, and was the sacrifice for your own selfish gain or was it for the betterment of your marriage? Have you submitted yourself to the Lord as a living sacrifice so that he can use you in your marriage or use your marriage as an example to show a world that the constitution of marriage will work and does not have to end in divorce?

Virtuous Assessment

1. Make a list of things that are of great value to you, that you could sacrifice to make your marriage more fulfilling.

2. Of that list, choose at least one of those items (to start with) and present it as a sacrifice unto the Lord.

3. Ask the Lord to accept your sacrifice as a deed to perform a service pleasing unto Him. This is between you and the Lord.

4. Watch God move!!! Within the next three months, see if your husband notices a difference and watch your relationship with Christ flourish.

Chapter 12

Can I Be a Silly Wife?

Just as we concluded the single ladies section of this book with examples of how you can be single and silly, I thought it would be good to give you some examples of how there have been some silly wife scenarios.

Sapphria

After Jesus had risen from the dead, He spent time with the Apostles. He shared with them things that would occur and how they should go out into the world to compel people to change their way of living. He would not send them without His Holy Spirit. Jesus then ascended up into heaven before the eyes of the Apostles. The Spirit of God could not be sent back to live within us, until Jesus had taken His rightful place on the right hand of His father. The book of Acts talks about the work (or acts) of the Apostles and how they went forth with power (after the Holy Ghost was descended), preaching and teaching repentance and baptism. During this time the Apostles ensured that the congregation's needs were met as all people had all things in common. No one had more or less than the other (Acts 4:32-37), some selling possessions, land, etc., so that everyone had what they needed.

There was this married couple by the name of Ananias and Sapphira. They sold one of their possessions but decided not to give all the money they received for that possession. The Bible says they sold "a" possession, which is singular and means they had more, but chose to sell one so that distribution to the necessity of others could continue. They both agreed that they would say (if asked) they only received a certain amount of money and would not tell the full amount for selling the "possession." Ananias, the husband, brought the money to Peter and laid it at his feet.

Listen, God is not stupid. Just as Satan requires a "body" or someone so that he can use them for his purpose, God does as well. The Holy Spirit persuaded Peter to ask Ananias about the money and if he had given it all. Peter discerned, by the Spirit, that Ananias had not given all the money and asked him why he was lying. Peter let Ananias know: "Hey listen; you didn't lie to me. You lied to God." Ananias died on the spot! People that saw were astonished. Other men rose up, wrapped him and carried him out to bury him. Meanwhile, three hours later Sapphira, the wife, walks in, not knowing what has occurred. Peter asks her the same question. She repeats the amount she and her husband agreed to state. Guess what? She died on the spot, too.

CHILEPLEASE!!! Wives, listen. God said in His word we will give an account of what we do in our own bodies and how we live this life unto Him. Yes we are one flesh when we wed – but honey, don't you be silly!!! Hmph! If your husband doesn't want to honor the Lord and live according to His word, you better walk that much closer to God because guess what? A lot of the blessings and favor of the Lord are from your husband obtaining you as his wife *annnyywayyy*. When or if he decides living for the Lord is not working for Him, you continue to do a work well pleasing to the Lord so that your children and your household don't lose out on the blessings of God. Chileplease! First of all…Sapphira should have stood boldly on the word. Listen, it's because of the Lord that you have received blessings, and then you can't stand to give one of your measly possessions to help someone else? How selfish. No, if I die, it won't be for someone else's foolishness. Wives, God cannot stand a liar. He said a liar cannot even be in his presence. God said he HATES a liar (Proverbs 6:16-17). It's not that you can't get forgiveness for lying, but isn't it just easier to tell the truth?

Listen, God knows if you're being dishonest about paying your tithes AND offerings. He can't trust you to pay a tenth of your earnings and an offering (which is just that…what you "offer")? You mean to tell me if you make $1,000 before taxes every two weeks, you can't give the Lord $100? Do you really think He needs your money? Did that $100 help you over the hump? Or were you still lacking? And you wonder why you are still struggling and you have a degree with a salary.

Paying tithes and offerings is not for God – it's for you to receive the blessings of God and again, to ensure the needs of the church aren't lacking. If the man or woman of God is not doing right by the money being given, they will have to give an account of that and believe me, God will expose them. I believe giving has become such a sore thumb because we mostly hear of people asking money for oil and prayer cloths and handkerchiefs.

Honestly, if I didn't have a church home and decided to turn on the television to get the Word, I would become horribly discouraged. The kingdom of God is not meat and drink. It's not about things. Yes, God says he wants us to prosper and HE will prosper us but begging…God ain't never begged anybody. Your giving should be free will. Meaning hey, you are free to give, but if you don't want to give, you know the consequences. You need to give into some ministry that's teaching the Word so that your blessings aren't hindered. I've taken time on this scenario because it really gets to me and irks me, how we see people begging for money and after the offering is raised, you are STILL asking for $10 and $20. Really?

God doesn't have to beg for anything. In fact, even when we decided to give our lives to Christ, He gave us a choice. Sure, the choice was, live for me and you get life or you die, but it was a choice still…I digress…But don't allow yourself to fall short and come up short because someone else is doing wrong and using God's people for selfish gain. You may have gone to college and obtained your degree, but sweetie if the Lord didn't open your understanding to retain the information presented to you in the classroom, you wouldn't have a degree. Surely, if He didn't touch the heart of the interviewer to bring you in for the interview or the manager to hire you, would not have gotten the job.

Don't be like Sapphira; shucks, we have enough struggles now as it is. We don't need any added struggles. Let me tell you something and I know my husband feels the same way as I do…you let someone in my household stop paying tithes and offerings. We are going to have to have a real conversation. What you are saying then is that you don't trust God. That means you don't believe the Word and we don't agree. So how can we walk together if we don't agree? I'm going to pay more than I'm supposed to, and not because I'm looking for a return but because the Lord deserves that and much more. He deserves our obedience. In fact, God said he'd rather we'd be obedient because it's better than our sacrifice. Weeelll…part of being obedient is doing what He says to do. You can't just pick and choose in the Bible what you want to do or pick a scripture that suits you. Wives, please don't be silly with your finances. You can be blessed today and laid off tomorrow.

Wives…just don't be silly!

Bathsheba

There's a story in the Bible about a man named King David. He became ruler over Israel as He was chosen by God to be so. We won't get into his story. One evening, David got out of his bed and went on his rooftop. It was there he spotted a beautiful woman bathing. Her name was Bathsheba. So he sent men to find out who this woman was. The messengers came back and told him Bathsheba was married to Uriah, who was away fighting in a war. That didn't deter David. He sent for her and Bathsheba monkey self went to David's house and committed adultery with him. She soon learned that she was pregnant.

During these times, if a woman was found to have committed adultery, both she and the man would be stoned to death. So imagine what went through her head as she could not try to pass the child off on her hubby because he wasn't there. So, Bathsheba told David and of course the king came up with a plan. He decided to call Uriah up from war so he would go home and be with his wife. King David learned from his messengers that Uriah would not go home. Uriah's beliefs were that he refused to be resting and in peace while his fellow soldiers were on the front line and thus he would not. So, when that plan failed, King David sought to have Uriah killed by putting him on the front line in the war and thus Uriah died. So, Bathsheba wouldn't be killed, marries the king, their child dies but then she gives birth to a son whom God loved dearly, Solomon. Bathsheba had some silly ways though.

Wives, okay, let's give her the benefit of the doubt, or at least try to. Maybe because David was a king, she was fearful of what he could do to her or her husband. After all, her husband was fighting in the war, as if that wasn't enough stress. You know what? I can't do it. Bathsheba was silly. Here's why that excuse doesn't work (her husband died anyway…). God has power over all flesh! Countless times have we seen scenarios when men and women of God have STOOD on the promises and principles of God regardless of the outcome and the outcome was favorable for them? Wives, most time the downfall of a man is a woman. What if we stand for the truth? What are you afraid of? Who are you afraid of? You have the almighty God AND his angels keeping charge over you to protect you. When King David sent his messengers and when Bathsheba went and saw what he wanted, she should have turned the other way. David knew who the Lord was and I just believe He would have been convicted. When you are a child of God, HE WILL PROTECT YOU!

Then she had to deal with the shame of pregnancy. Do you know why? It wasn't because of HER sin. All that the Lord did for King David and choosing him as king…see, the Bible talks about what's done in the dark will come to the light but it's not because that person did wrong. It has to come to light so God can show others…."Hey; this person says they representing me…that's not me! Those aren't my ways, my actions, my thoughts." You become a stumbling block and then the ministry becomes blamed. People turned their backs on the Lord because of those who are not representing Christ. You better believe honey they will give an account. Oh yeah, God has to let the world know…WHAT THEY ARE DOING IS NOT OF ME! I AM NOT THAT KIND OF GOD! I AM NOT THE AUTHOR OF CONFUSION!

Wives don't be silly. Please don't commit adultery against your husband. There's no temptation that can overtake us or come upon us that we cannot avoid. Even with the temptation, the Lord will make a way for us to get out of it. Is it worth losing your family or even losing your place in Christ? Yes, God is a forgiving God and His mercy and grace covers us, but please don't take Him for granted.

Job's Wife

On countless times we have heard about the story of Job and the sufferings he endured. Job was the richest man in the east, had the prettiest children, ten of them in fact, and many possessions. However, Job went through a suffering like no other. He lost all ten of his children, had boils on his flesh, flesh fell from his bones, breath stank and his friends even talked about him. How often does Satan use the ones closest to us to discourage us? His wife comes to him and basically says, "How can you still hold your integrity in God? Why don't you just choose the quickest way out to end your suffering by cursing God and dying? Then you don't have to suffer." Of course, Job put her in her place and told her, "Hey, the Lord makes who he wants to make rich and who he wants to make poor (I'm still paraphrasing here), but I will still bless His name."

Wives, how often have our husband's been in an uncomfortable situation, a test of faith with the mother of their child from a previous relationship or issues on the job, and instead of encouraging our spouses we begin to complain and murmur? Don't be silly like Job's wife. Nowhere does it state that his wife prayed unto the Lord on her husband's behalf. In fact, her blessings were because of Job since he was the covering and he did honor the Lord. It was Job who feared God (again not saying his wife didn't), it was Job who avoided evil, it was Job that walked upright and perfect before God, it was Job who continually put his children before the Lord, sacrificing to God on their behalf. Wives, when "things" don't go well in our lives, let's not be hasty to make quick judgments and decisions. We should get with our spouses and go before the Lord on the behalf of the family. We must remember who made us. When we go before the Lord, God is not moved by our many words and crying, anger, emotion…none of that moves God. He doesn't take pleasure in seeing us suffer for doing wrong and desires to help us. Listen, God saw his own son, Jesus, suffer for things He did not do, all for our sakes. He sees through all of that sobbing and snotting! God is moved by our faith and that's how God moved on Job's behalf. God knew Job trusted Him. Who do you believe in? What do you stand for?

Eve

Oh boy! We get to…the mother of them all. I say Eve is the silliest wife of all time. So in the beginning, God created everything and created Adam. He gave Adam the power to name every creature on the Earth. Then God saw that Adam needed some help and He put Adam to sleep, made Eve from Adam's rib and brought Eve to him. They lived in paradise and could speak to God PERSONALLY AND ON A DAILY BASIS!! Before Eve was made, God gave Adam the commandment about the tree of knowledge of good and evil and not to eat of it.

Okay…here comes Satan! He approaches Eve to eat off the tree that God forbade them to eat of. Surely Adam told her about the commandment because she said she wasn't supposed to or else they would die. Satan tells her, yes you can, and you won't die. You'll just be like little gods. As if living in a paradise weren't enough (and what in the HELLO did Eve need with more knowledge anyway), she was enticed and gave in to the temptation and ate the fruit. Then her monkey self gave some to Adam as well. Listen, Eve didn't give up the garden for "milk and cookies" or even for money (which she didn't need anyway). She gave it up for MORE KNOWLEDGE? To become like God, so she thought? What was she going to do more than God had already done? As I sit here in my fifth month of pregnancy with my first son, fourth biological child, fifth overall…ooh if I could have a conversation with Eve, I would say: "Jesus, is that Eve over there? Can I talk to her? Girl, what were you thinking? Are you serious? Do you realize all we had to go through to get back to paradise and you were already in it? You listened to the serpent…that you did not know and here you were taken from this man's rib and you couldn't take heed to what your husband told you GOD told him? You were in a paradise…what more did you need, lady?"

Then the three of them, Adam, Eve and the serpent began blaming one another. Adam blamed Eve because she gave him the fruit…Eve said the snake tricked her…God punished everybody. Adam had to work with his hands and labor to provide. Eve monkey self added much sorrow to child birthing experience and husbands were to rule over their wives. Don't believe me:

> *Unto the woman he said, I will greatly multiply thy sorrow and thy conception; in sorrow thou shalt bring forth children; and thy desire shall be to thy husband, and he shall rule over thee. (Genesis 3:16)*

THANKS, EVE! Wives, Eve made a quick and hasty decision without consulting her husband. When you marry, any decision made should be discussed and implemented as one because you are one. Don't make a decision and then tell your husband about it or he finds out. It's only going to cause confusion in your relationship. What could've been a small issue or a non-issue now becomes a problem that causes one of the two of you to end up on the couch.

Part 3

Every Woman

Chapter 13

Forgiveness

There's one subject that we did not address, which leads us to becoming virtuous; that subject is forgiveness. Jesus talks about forgiveness and it is so important that we perform this act!

Forgiveness is not so that you and that person can reconcile and mend the relationship (if that occurs, then that's an added bonus). Forgiveness is for you to be able to move on with your life.

Have you ever gotten into an altercation with someone and you parted ways in a negative manner? You know (and they know also) the person wronged you, but you're being treated as if you're at fault. Then, when you see that person again, they appear as if they've moved on and are happy; however, inwardly you want to see them hurting and quite frankly, you are angered even more. Remember this: "He who angers you, controls you." When you and that person are in the same setting, you allow them to control the environment because your entire mood changes, your attitude changes and in fact, you are ready to leave the event. You suddenly begin replaying the incident that once occurred, in your mind – you are not in control anymore.

God said it's okay to be angry, but don't have anger:

> *Be ye angry, and sin not: let not the sun go down upon your wrath… (Ephesians 4:26)*

When you're angry, it's a temporary feeling of hurt and frustration; but you're able to move on. When you are angered, it's something that's deeply rooted and can turn into a malicious act of violence or hatred towards the other person. Here's what God said about anger:

> *Cease from anger, and forsake wrath: fret not thyself in any wise to do evil. (Psalms 37:8)*

> *A soft answer turneth away wrath: but grievous words stir up anger. (Proverbs 15:1)*

> *Let all bitterness, and wrath, and anger, and clamour, and evil speaking, be put away from you, with all malice: And be ye kind one to another, tenderhearted, forgiving one another, even as God for Christ's sake hath forgiven you. (Ephesians 4:31-32)*

Forgiveness frees you from hurt, abandonment, lies and control by others. Forgiveness sometimes takes time, depending on the situation; it's part of our healing process, to become strong and virtuous. If God is ready to forgive and we say that we have put on his characteristics, then we must also be ready to forgive:

> *For thou, Lord, art good, and ready to forgive; and plenteous in mercy unto all them that call upon thee. (Psalms 86:5)*

Forgive….

If your husband was unfaithful, forgive him. It was his loss because listen, a virtuous woman (you'll soon learn) is hard to find. As long as you kept your commitment to God, held your integrity and did a service well pleasing to Him (the Lord), you can press your shoulders back, stand up tall, and hold your head up high.

Forgive…

If you experienced being violated through molestation or rape, forgive. Satan tried to use that person to take your strength and courage, not knowing it only made you stronger and powerful; and now since you have peace in God, you are a new creature anyway – you didn't die; YOU MULTIPLIED! Your pain had a purpose.

There's someone who is not as strong as you were, to get through it alone;

There's someone that you will need to show love to because they don't feel love;

There's someone who will need your strength and testimony;

There's someone who will need healing and can receive it through your guidance;

There's someone who will need you to catch them from falling into a state of depression and suicide, because you know all too well how it feels.

Forgive…

If you were abandoned by one or both of your parents, forgive them. Through it all, you learned that God your Father was there, protecting you from unforeseen danger and He NEVER left you…

…I will never leave thee, nor forsake thee. (Hebrews 13:5)

One misconception is that when you forgive, you forget. NO! You don't forget. You don't forget because you may have to share your testimony to help free another woman. You may need to remember so that if the path you had taken caused self-hurt, you don't revisit it again. You may need to remember to LOOK YOUR ENEMY DIRECTLY IN THE FACE AND SAY: "I KNOW…I REMEMBER…BUT I FORGIVE YOU; and I will ask the Lord to forgive you because you didn't understand what you did!"

And when ye stand praying, forgive, if ye have ought against any: that your Father also which is in heaven may forgive you your trespasses (Mark 11:25)

Look upon mine affliction and my pain; and forgive all my sins. O keep my soul, and deliver me: let me not be ashamed; for I put my trust in thee. (Psalms 25:18, 20)

Chapter 14

Potentially Silly Questions & the Virtuous Answers

1. My husband has hit me before but I know he is a good man and can be better if he changes his life. I want to leave him but I'm scared and I don't want anyone else to be with him. What should I do?

As before stated, the topic of abuse, whether physical or emotional, from anyone is one that cannot be taken lightly. Recall we talked about learned behaviors. When abuse occurs, especially during childhood, it shapes a person's character and becomes a part of who that person develops in to. Although I have never experienced it, such abuse is not acceptable. In the context of the Bible, God said:

> *But whoso shall offend one of these little ones which believe in me, it were better for him that a millstone were hanged about his neck, and that he were drowned in the depth of the sea. (Matthew 18:6)*

When someone offends you, it means that person has attacked you or insulted you in some sort of way. Here Jesus is calling us his little children. Whether you have been living for

Christ for years, or just recently accepted Him as your personal savior, if someone does anything to you, Jesus said it were better if that person were hung and drowned in the sea. When you offend one of God's children, you offend or hurt Him and that is ever dangerous. Fear is torment; when you live in fear of what someone can do to you, you're not free. Our God would not be a just God to allow someone to cause us harm and to be bound when He gives us freedom, if you have His protection. There is NO WAY that Satan will have dominion of God's people. We GIVE him control but when you totally commit your life to Christ, He will NOT allow harm to come near you.

If a man hit you once and he has not made any effort to change his life for the better, he will hit you again. I can't tell you what to do, but I know Jesus said He will make a way for you to escape any situation. Those conditions of fear and torment are not acceptable for anyone to experience. Would you want your children to see you being abused and feeling helpless? Then they grow up and learn that behavior and they either become abused or abuse others because of what they have experienced in their life. You're also concerned about seeing this man with someone else. What's more important to you; your life or this man? Anything we put before God will become our downfall. You may say it's not that easy and no one understands. Jesus understands abuse. He didn't wrong anyone yet he took piercings, beatings, and nails in his flesh, but for our sakes so we can experience peace in Him. Please ladies, don't let Jesus's suffering be in vain in your life. He loves you move than you know and is waiting with open arms to be your protection, provider and confidant. Take refuge in Jesus and He will keep you:

> *He that dwelleth in the secret place of the most High shall abide under the shadow of the Almighty. I will say of the LORD, He is my refuge and my fortress: my God; in him*

> *will I trust. Surely he shall deliver thee from the snare of the fowler, and from the noisome pestilence. He shall cover thee with his feathers, and under his wings shalt thou trust: his truth shall be thy shield and buckler. Because thou hast made the LORD, which is my refuge, even the most High, thy habitation; There shall no evil befall thee, neither shall any plague come nigh thy dwelling. For he shall give his angels charge over thee, to keep thee in all thy ways. (Psalms 91:1-4, 9-11)*

Regardless of how you are threatened or attacked, believe me God sees it all and the Lord will take care of your enemies.

> *For evildoers shall be cut off: but those that wait upon the LORD, they shall inherit the earth. For yet a little while, and the wicked shall not be: yea, thou shalt diligently consider his place, and it shall not be. But the meek shall inherit the earth; and shall delight themselves in the abundance of peace. The wicked plotteth against the just, and gnasheth upon him with his teeth. The LORD shall laugh at him: for he seeth that his day is coming. The wicked have drawn out the sword, and have bent their bow, to cast down the poor and needy, and to slay such as be of upright conversation. Their sword shall enter into their own heart, and their bows shall be broken. (Psalms 37:9-15)*

If there are children involved and you are afraid of this coward (yes, I called him a coward because in most scenarios a man's physical strength is more powerful than a woman's and even that much more if alcohol or drugs and involved), there is help. If you need to speak to someone about protection and devising a plan, call the National Domestic Violence Hotline (800-799-7233). As hurtful as it may be, talk to your family to have a safe haven for your children. If you're in the midst of abuse, call 9-1-1. You don't know what this man is capable of. If he has no regard for you or your children, to hit you in their presence, he's subject to do more and that's the reality. Get help if not for you, for your children's sake.

2. I have a boyfriend and we have had a great relationship for the past two years. There is just one major issue: he is married. I love him and he says he is going to leave his wife, but if he does that I wouldn't want to be with him because I like not being committed. Should I stay with him?

Ok ladies…how can the relationship be "great" and it's built upon dishonesty, selfishness and distrust? If those are your morals and beliefs then it probably is great; but I believe that you are hiding behind this situation for other reasons. You feel you are getting what you want, but honey he is using you as well. Have you ever heard of herpes, AIDS, syphilis? You can't tell me that when he leaves you to return home, you don't feel lonely or depressed or wonder what he's doing at home with his FAMILY! You can't convince me that this is the life you expect to have from now on and you have peace with it! How would you feel if you found out that your dad had a secret affair with someone else? No doubt that would devastate your mother, but you as the child would be devastated as well, hurt, resentful and angry.

What if this man has children? What did this lady do to deserve disrespect from you? Whatever you put out or do to others WILL come back to you. If this man leaves his wife for you, don't think he won't leave you for someone else. Better yet, how do you not know there isn't more than one woman on the side? Is this how you value yourself? You believe this is your worth? Remember the words of God and He cannot lie.

Yes, He wants to see us blessed but there are repercussions for being deceitful:

> *Therefore judge nothing before the appointed time; wait until the Lord comes. He will bring to light what is hidden in darkness and will expose the motives of the heart. (I Corinthians 4:5)*

When your deeds become exposed, do you think you have a right to be angry? Right away what do most women do? Get in a heated debate with the wife. Really…what right do you have? In the Old Testament, the man and woman caught in the act of adultery would be stoned to death and this would be acceptable in the eyesight of God. Ladies, He is the same God; he does not change. No we don't get stoned, but we suffer in many other ways that feel like death.

> *And the man that committeth adultery with another man's wife, even he that committeth adultery with his neighbour's wife, the adulterer and the adulteress shall surely be put to death. (Leviticus 20:10)*

> *But whoso committeth adultery with a woman lacketh understanding: he that doeth it destroyeth his own soul. (Proverbs 6:32)*

> *But these, as natural brute beasts, made to be taken and destroyed, speak evil of the things that they understand not; and shall utterly perish in their own corruption; Having eyes full of adultery, and that cannot cease from sin; beguiling unstable souls: an heart they have exercised with covetous practices; cursed children: Which have forsaken the right way, and are gone astray…(2 Peter 2:12, 14-15)*

3. I live with my children's dad and we have been together for four years. I have recently given my life to Christ and I'm trying to do the right thing. He says he's going to marry me but again it's been four years. When we make a date to get married, something always happens. He gets angry with me or he says we already live as a married couple and don't need rings to make it official. I don't want to leave him in fear that my children won't have a relationship with him if I do. Sometimes, in the midst of our debates, he even tells me I should leave. What should I do?

Honey, listen: LEAVE!!! It's been four years and he's looking for a reason to not marry you. Actually, what it sounds like is that he's stringing you along so you don't leave him and he doesn't have to pay child support; but if he's encouraged you to leave, he does not want you. Why put yourself through this? You can make it without this man. You deserve better than this! He's probably not going to marry you! Don't compromise your beliefs for a man. I keep saying this, but whatever you put before God, will become your god and your downfall. One thing is for certain, God will not take a back seat to anyone. Don't put your life on hold for this man! Since you have committed your life to Christ you are your children's covering. That means they will be blessed (or not) by your actions and living by the principles of Christ. Your help comes from the Lord, not from a man! Let the Lord (your husband) provide for you.

> *I will lift up mine eyes unto the hills, from whence cometh my help. My help cometh from the LORD, which made heaven and earth. He will not suffer thy foot to be moved: he that keepeth thee will not slumber. Behold, he that keepeth Israel shall neither slumber nor sleep. The LORD is thy keeper: the LORD is thy shade upon thy right hand. The sun shall not smite thee by day, nor the moon by night.*

The LORD shall preserve thee from all evil: he shall preserve thy soul. The LORD shall preserve thy going out and thy coming in from this time forth, and even for evermore. (Psalms 121:1-8)

For thy Maker is thine husband; the LORD of hosts is his name; and thy Redeemer the Holy One of Israel; The God of the whole earth shall he be called. (Isaiah 54:5)

I have been young, and now am old; yet have I not seen the righteous forsaken, nor his seed begging bread. He is ever merciful, and lendeth; and his seed is blessed. Depart from evil, and do good; and dwell for evermore. (Psalms 37:25-27)

4. My husband and I have had issues in our marriage. I have on occasion confided in my family who says I should divorce him; we have both recently dedicated our lives to Christ but I'm torn because when we are around my family there is so much tension. What do I do?

Honey, we discussed this in the marriage section of the book. When you married your husband, you married HIM! You did not marry his family. Yes, you gained another mother and dad and siblings through marriage, but they should not become the decision makers in your household. Bringing a family into your intimate moments of marriage or any uncomfortable situations complicates your marriage. Quite naturally your family wants what's best for you, but they don't provide food and shelter to you and your household. At the end of the day, when you can no longer provide financial support for your family and they get an attitude with you, who will you run to? When you both gave your life to Christ, old things are passed and all things are new. That means whatever happened in the past, you decided to leave it there and move forward. Satan's job is to rekindle that anger and he often uses those closest to us. Instead of encouraging you to stay together and to see you happy, they discourage your union. So whom are you living for? At some point you will have to say to your family forgive me; I invited you into a personal space in my marriage and I should have not. You will have to express to your family your genuine love for them but when you decided to marry your husband you decided to forsake all except Jesus Christ and you both have decided to let Him control your life!

> *Therefore if any man be in Christ, he is a new creature: old things are passed away; behold, all things are become new. (2 Corinthians 5:17)*

5. I confess Christ as my personal Savior and I am single but I want to be married. Is it wrong to date? How can I learn or meet someone if I don't date that person?

Ladies, what do you define as dating? What are you seeking for? Here is my belief:

> *Delight thyself also in the LORD: and he shall give thee the desires of thine heart. Commit thy way unto the LORD; trust also in him; and he shall bring it to pass. (Psalms 37:5-6)*

I can only talk about what worked for me. I tried my way for so long and when I made Jesus my all and put Him first, He knew that He could trust me in that if he gave me a husband, I would continue to stand boldly on his Word, come what may. I desired to be married and I stated my desire to the Lord, but I had to patiently wait for Him to move on my behalf and on His time.

> *I waited patiently for the LORD; and he inclined unto me, and heard my cry. (Psalms 40:1)*

We think we know when we are ready but we really don't. Why not trust in someone who knows all of our thoughts and intentions?

> *For the word of God is quick, and powerful, and sharper than any two-edged sword, piercing even to the dividing asunder of soul and spirit, and of the joints and marrow, and is a discerner of the thoughts and intents of the heart. (Hebrews 4:12)*

He knows if a man has ulterior motives or is seeking to please Him (Him being Jesus). We can only take the information that a man has given us and try to decipher if he is being sincere or if he's being deceitful. For me, I felt life was too short to be playing games. I had been played with enough and been played and been stupid enough to wait on the Lord and let Him guide me.

6. *I am a single woman who has been living for Christ for the past three years. I met a man through a mutual acquaintance about two weeks ago and I believe he is the one. I must admit that I did give in to my temptation and we were intimate but I just believe he is the one! Can I marry him and still obtain God's favor? Can we have a holy matrimony?* Ladies, here is the issue. You didn't deny yourself.

> *Then said Jesus unto his disciples, If any man will come after me, let him deny himself, and take up his cross, and follow me (Matthew 16:24)*

Jesus is saying if you choose to follow Him, you have to deny your own desires and selfish ways, bear whatever burdens and sufferings you must face in life, and make it happen! Follow Him at all cost! What happen is that you gave in to your fleshly desires and it had been soooo long (let's keep it real and G-rated) and he touched a part of you that hadn't been touched in three years. Now that the "itch" has been scratched, your flesh desires that feeling again and so you have an inward battle. It's like you're having a discussion with yourself. Your spiritual man is saying: "You have been down this road. How can you let yourself down and Jesus down? You know where he brought you from and going back to this is starting your process all over again. How could you?" Your fleshly (or carnal) man is saying: "I can't help it; I'm a woman and I have desires. How do I control the feelings that God has given me? He gave me these feelings?" Listen, when you give your life to the Lord, He doesn't take our desires for us but He gives us wisdom and knowledge to control ourselves…to bring ourselves under subjection.

> *But I keep under my body, and bring it into subjection: lest that by any means, when I have preached to others, I myself should be a castaway. (I Corinthians 9:27)*

> *Blessed is the man that endureth temptation: for when he is tried, he shall receive the crown of life, which the Lord hath promised to them that love him. Let no man say when he is tempted, I am tempted of God: for God cannot be tempted with evil, neither tempteth he any man: But every man is tempted, when he is drawn away of his own lust, and enticed. Then when lust hath conceived, it bringeth forth sin: and sin, when it is finished, bringeth forth death. Do not err, my beloved brethren. (James 1:12-16)*

This goes for women as well. YOU have to do that. If you put forth the effort, then the Lord will help you. You can't sit back and say Lord take this away. No! Jesus said He gave us the power! Use your power. Come out from among the people and things that make you go against the Word of God. Jesus said He will then receive you:

> *Wherefore come out from among them, and be ye separate, saith the Lord, and touch not the unclean thing; and I will receive you. (2 Corinthians 6:17)*

There is no sin in the Lord. When you sin, you separate yourself from Him, his protection, His assurances:

> *Behold, the LORD's hand is not shortened, that it cannot save; neither his ear heavy, that it cannot hear: But your iniquities have separated between you and your God, and your sins have hid his face from you, that he will not hear. For your hands are defiled with blood, and your fingers with iniquity; your lips have spoken lies, your tongue hath muttered perverseness. (Isaiah 59:1-3)*

Jesus said those that God gave to Him, NO MAN is able to pluck them (or take them) out of His hand. You belong to Him. When you give in to temptation, don't stay there and waddle in it. Get up, dust yourself off, sincerely ask for forgiveness and move forward. He told us all have sinned and come short, but don't use that as an excuse to continue to do wrong. When you know to do good and you don't, that's sin and once again, you place more separation between you and the Lord:

> *Therefore to him that knoweth to do good, and doeth it not, to him it is sin. (James 4:17)*

Whatever caused you to deny Jesus, you need to RUN from it! Because you are running for your life – and your life is worth more than just milk and cookies!

7. I am single living for the Lord. Is it okay that when I have an "itch," I have "Jake" take care of me? I'm not sinning because I'm not with a man, just fulfilling my desires so I do not commit fornication. Is that wrong?

Women, you're still seeking to please your flesh and fulfill your lustful desires. Do you think the Lord will dwell in your temple performing this type of act? If you didn't think it was wrong, why do you feel convicted after the fact? You are performing acts based on your sinful nature. Here's what Jesus said:

> *This I say then, Walk in the Spirit, and ye shall not fulfill the lust of the flesh. For the flesh lusteth against the Spirit, and the Spirit against the flesh: and these are contrary the one to the other: so that ye cannot do the things that ye would. But if ye be led of the Spirit, ye are not under the law. Now the works of the flesh are manifest, which are these; Adultery, fornication, uncleanness, lasciviousness, Idolatry, witchcraft, hatred, variance, emulations, wrath, strife, seditions, heresies, Envyings, murders, drunkenness, revellings, and such like: of the which I tell you before, as I have also told you in time past, that they which do such things shall not inherit the kingdom of God. (Galatians 5:16-21).*

You are performing an act of lasciviousness which is simply a lustful pleasure. In NO way are you enhancing your spiritual life. Jesus says those that perform these types of acts will NOT inherit (inherit simply means you have a right to obtain) the kingdom of God. You may ask: "What is the kingdom of God?"

> *For the kingdom of God is not meat and drink; but righteousness, and peace, and joy in the Holy Ghost. (Romans 14:17)*

So you will not have the right to obtain righteousness (which is the freedom from guilt or sin), peace and joy? Aren't these the intangible things we seek and desire to have because we didn't have them? You're willing to give up your inheritance for your own self-pleasure? Is it really worth it? If you desire to be married or can't contain yourself, talk to your Heavenly Father. He knows what you need before you ask, but be careful what you ask for!

8. *I was married but I am no longer; I feel lonely and desire to be married again. What should I do?*

Continue to do what Jesus said:

> *But seek ye first the kingdom of God, and his righteousness; and all these things shall be added unto you. (Matthew 6:33)*

You can't get weary in your well-doing and then complain when the Lord doesn't move in YOUR time frame. We don't think or act like Him; he knows what's best and when it's best.

> *For my thoughts are not your thoughts, neither are your ways my ways, saith the LORD. For as the heavens are higher than the earth, so are my ways higher than your ways, and my thoughts than your thoughts. (Isaiah 55:8-9)*

Maybe He has you in a place where He can have your undivided attention for you to focus on Him, get some priorities straightened in your life and learn yourself and who you are. Whatever the reason that you are no longer married, whether unfaithfulness or death (widower), everything happens for a reason. Evaluate your past situation, see what areas you can improve upon, and do that. You're not alone if you're in Christ; you may feel alone because a physical person isn't there, but ladies, don't define who you are based upon being in a relationship.

9. I am up in age (50+) and men are my weakness. I have never been married but I want to be. I been waiting on the Lord and I want one now! Is that wrong?

There's a reason you are in a "holding" state. Have you been starting your process all over again with God? Meaning, do you do well for a while and then when temptation comes, you give in and have to start your process all over again? Does the Lord know if He can trust you? A man can only do to you what you allow. Do you place yourself in high-esteem to demand respect and not be disrespected and used by a man? If the Lord grants you your desires, will you place that man before God? There's no age restriction on marriage. Most of us desire companionship. The Lord made marriage for us; when we get to heaven, there will be no marriage:

> *For in the resurrection they neither marry, nor are given in marriage, but are as the angels of God in heaven. (Matthew 22:30)*

Don't give up on God; He knows what's best for you and he knows your sincerity and your commitment to Him as well:

> *O lord, thou hast searched me, and known me. Thou knowest my downsitting and mine uprising, thou understandest my thought afar off. Thou compassest my path and my lying down, and art acquainted with all my ways. For there is not a word in my tongue, but, lo, O LORD, thou knowest it altogether. (Psalms 139:1-4)*

Be patient:

> *My brethren, count it all joy when ye fall into divers temptations; Knowing this, that the trying of your faith worketh patience. But let patience have her perfect work, that ye may be perfect and entire, wanting nothing. (James 1:2-4)*

10. I've been hurt so much by men that I've decided that I will be with women. It seems only right, since I am a woman and being with a woman, she will understand me; plus I wouldn't have to worry about getting pregnant. No one can judge me!

You're right that no one can judge you; the Bible says, that everyone shall give account of himself to God (Romans 14:12). If you're not seeking to please the Lord and you are a lesbian, and then do what makes you happy; but if you are confessing to be a Christian, God destroyed an entire nation because of unnatural affection. So much has been made in the church world about homosexuality. We often hear some preaching heavily against it, but then when their deeds are reproved, the same things they fought against, they are found doing. Listen! God loves us and desires us to know the truth. We need to be held accountable and told not just why this goes against the Word of God, but also shown in the Bible and why He has no pleasure in these types of acts. So often, those who have a stronghold of homosexuality are kicked out of the one place they should find refuge and deliverance. It's sin! Sin is sin; as long as that person has not lied on God (blasphamed), they can get forgiveness and deliverance because Jesus loves us all and came that we might know the truth so we can be made free. Jesus said:

> *Wherefore God also gave them up to uncleanness through the lusts of their own hearts, to dishonour their own bodies between themselves: Who changed the truth of God into a lie, and worshipped and served the creature more than the Creator, who is blessed for ever. Amen. For this cause God gave them up unto vile affections: for even their women did change the natural use into that which is against nature: And likewise also the men, leaving the natural use of the woman, burned in their lust one toward another; men with men working that which is unseemly, and receiving in themselves that recompence of their error which was meet. And even as they did not like to retain God in their knowledge, God gave them over to a reprobate mind, to do those things which are not convenient; (Romans 1:24-28)*

When we begin to no longer acknowledge God and recognize Him for who He is, people turn to their own desires, burning in their lust toward one another. Lust is filth; it is not pure. Our sins separate us from Christ. He doesn't know sin and will not dwell in impurities. Think about the question stated. Since this woman has been hurt by men, her plans were to turn to women. What was her realization? Could there have been sexual abuse that occurred in her past which caused hurt, shame and pain, insomuch that she no longer desires to have any dealings with a man? Or could it have been her not being built up by the women in her circle who did not encourage her and uplift her and help her realize that she is beautiful on the inside and out? What this means to me is that this person is seeking love in the wrong places and only setting herself up for failure because she's going about it the wrong way. A person can be defined as insane when they continue to do the same things over and over thinking their results will change. Whether with a man or a woman, the end result is conflict, hurt and anguish. Let's not look for a quick fix to our problems. It's time to find the root and destroy it! Whatever is controlling your life in a negative manner and preventing you from being free, it's time to let it go!

Conclusion

Women, here's where our thoughts become reality. Now is the time to take what we have learned and read and make it a reality; it's time for implementation and putting everything into action. As we draw near to the conclusion of this journey, there are some things we must do IF we feel a change is needed for us to become virtuous:

> 1. You were asked in the single ladies section to identify your reality. Go back and review that reality and confirm you have identified what event/events in your life caused you to be silly.
>
> 2. What commitment(s) will you make to prevent yourself from becoming silly again?
>
> 3. How will you hold yourself accountable to carry out this commitment (will you have a daily visual reminder or will you inform someone else of what you are doing so that person can assist with making you accountable)?
>
> 4. Again, with my experience, it takes at least three months to make something habit-forming, so for three months, move forward with the fulfillment of your commitment. If your commitment isn't realized by then, add an additional three months until your goal is reached; don't give up!

5. Share your story of success; your next task will be to pull another woman from depression and feelings of despair to success and virtuousness...pay it forward!!!

A Prayer for All Women

Father, I thank you that you have allowed me to write about topics that affect us, your daughters. Instead of being respected and loved we have been humiliated and sought out to be destroyed. But God, I thank you for sending your son, Jesus!

Jesus, I thank you that you loved us and cared about us to take us and bring us back to our first love, which is YOU! I thank you, Jesus, that we have begun to realize that sin has separated us from you and caused us to fail in carrying out your plan for our lives. But OH Jesus, we do know that all is not lost. For we have decided to re-commit ourselves unto YOU and to no longer allow sin to have control over our lives...whatever and whoever that may be. They cannot control our lives anymore; they CANNOT control our minds anymore; they CANNOT have our children anymore.

God, we thank you that you have allowed us to bear children. For we now know and understand the importance of us nurturing and teaching our children and oh Lord, not just our children but to stand up and be accountable such that when we see other women falling short and feeling helpless, we are able to be a light and to encourage them as well to continue on and to strive for success! We acknowledge that we have not been treating our children as if we are their "caretakers" but rather as their owners and we now know they belong to you. From this day forward, we will seek to be better caretakers by showing these children love, hope, faith, trust and peace because they are dependent upon us and if they don't receive it from us women, there will be a piece missing from their soul, to be sent into a cruel world where they will be left to learn on their own.

Lord, we ask for your forgiveness today, for seeking to please ourselves and not you! We know that if we please you, everything else will fall into place. For too long God, have we made the creation (man) and not the creator (you) first in our lives. We've done everything to obtain the attention of the man, yet we have become invisible to you because of our sin. Lord, we thank you that your grace and mercy have kept us and covered us all these years and now. We will no longer become reliant upon grace and mercy because we will be obedient to your word, which means we have established a relationship with you, you know us, and you live in us because we are not defiling our temple. We understand that our temple is your place of dwelling and we will keep it clean!

We didn't realize what love was until we began to realize how and why you loved us and we sincerely thank you! There's nothing that we did to deserve your unconditional love but now we realize what we can do is give it back by following in the steps of Jesus. We ask that you order our steps, Lord! Anything that is not like you, remove the desire and remove it altogether! We only have one life and we realize that our life is too important to be played with, muzzled over and taken advantage of.

This, Lord, may be new to some of us and Lord, by the words shown in this book...your words, we believe, but help our unbelief...we can't do this alone and we now know we are not alone. You said you would never leave us, but we left you and we are now returning to never let you down again. We are willing and ready to be a vessel used by you! This we pray in your son Jesus's name, Amen!

Epilogue

Throughout this book, we have discussed various scenarios that all women, single and married alike, may encounter. There were so many other issues and topics not discussed, but certainly not because they are of any lesser importance than the ones identified. Not all scenarios are the same and some may require resolutions not defined in this book. The intentions of this book are to focus on positive solutions and to encourage women to be accountable, confident, strong and firm in who you are! For example, there's absolutely no way a person can speak on the sensitive topic of physical and mental abuse if one hasn't experienced it; but one thing is for certain in any scenario: God's Word stands firm and He means what He says. He will never leave us nor forsake us and let any of us down. We have to learn not to let ourselves down or Him down.

Additionally throughout this book, references are made to the Word of God, Jesus and what his expectations of us are as people of God. I can only speak to what works for me. Before I accepted Jesus Christ as my personal Savior, I was a lost cause. My hope and inspiration came through Him; therefore, I can only speak on what I know has worked and continues to work for me. I cannot deny Him and will not under any circumstances. In no way is this book intended to cause division or to debate various religious beliefs. There is, however, one thing I have come to learn. The truth does two things: causes divisions and makes you free! Regardless of what your beliefs are, the principles of God can still be applied in all walks of life. We all can admit that we have had some silly moments in our lives if we still aren't being silly. It is therefore my prayer that you were able to grasp a piece of material from this book and apply it to your life so that we can turn from our silly ways and become virtuous women.

Finally, I'd like to leave you with this thought. God asked a question in the Bible of who can find a virtuous woman. What this implies to me is that if you have to "find" a virtuous woman (which simply means standing up for what's right, being honest and having good morals and standards) there aren't many woman using sound judgment. Can the Lord hold you accountable to be his virtuous child? Will you stand for the truth regardless if the outcome isn't favorable for you in the short run? Are you willing to sacrifice your own gain, to witness to the soul of a another woman and to lead her to esteem herself higher than she has? Who can find a virtuous woman? Here is how a silly woman becomes virtuous. Whether you are single and being a wife unto the Lord or you have been espoused to a man, the Word of God says in Proverbs 31:10-30:

> *Who can find a virtuous woman? for her price is far above rubies.*
>
> *The heart of her husband doth safely trust in her, so that he shall have no need of spoil.*
>
> *She will do him good and not evil all the days of her life.*
>
> *She seeketh wool, and flax, and worketh willingly with her hands.*

She is like the merchants' ships; she bringeth her food from afar.

She riseth also while it is yet night, and giveth meat to her household, and a portion to her maidens.

She considereth a field, and buyeth it: with the fruit of her hands she planteth a vineyard.

She girdeth her loins with strength, and strengtheneth her arms.

She perceiveth that her merchandise is good: her candle goeth not out by night.

She layeth her hands to the spindle, and her hands hold the distaff.

She stretcheth out her hand to the poor; yea, she reacheth forth her hands to the needy.

She is not afraid of the snow for her household: for all her household are clothed with scarlet.

She maketh herself coverings of tapestry; her clothing is silk and purple.

Her husband is known in the gates, when he sitteth among the elders of the land.

She maketh fine linen, and selleth it; and delivereth girdles unto the merchant.

Strength and honour are her clothing; and she shall rejoice in time to come.

She openeth her mouth with wisdom; and in her tongue is the law of kindness.

She looketh well to the ways of her household, and eateth not the bread of idleness.

Her children arise up, and call her blessed; her husband also, and he praiseth her.

Many daughters have done virtuously, but thou excellest them all.

Favour is deceitful, and beauty is vain: but a woman that feareth the LORD, she shall be praised.

About the Author

Kimberly Rochelle Lock was born August 23, 1975, in Milwaukee, Wisconsin. Being the only child of her mother, she was preserved. She was so fascinated with learning that at, the age of five during a blizzard, she walked to school only to find it closed. It was not uncommon for her to participate in statewide spelling bees. Since she was so advanced academically for her age, she began taking pre-college courses at the University of Wisconsin at the age of eleven. In her spare time she played basketball and musical instruments, such as the flute, baritone, harp, clarinet, and her favorite, the cello. Kim's charisma led her to be the first runner up as Ms. Teen Wisconsin Scholarship and Recognition Pageant at the age of fifteen.

Her personality was shaped by God. As a young girl, she loved going to church with her grandmother, who attended Lively Stone Deliverance Center in Milwaukee, Wisconsin. When the church traveled and visited other churches, as long as "granny" was going, Kim was going. She went so much with her grandmother that others began to think she was her grandmother's daughter.

After she graduated from Pulaski High School at the age of sixteen, the University of Wisconsin welcomed her as a student to pursue a Bachelor's Degree in Management Information Systems. Later, she completed her Master's Degree in Telecommunications Keller Graduate School of Management.

At the age of twenty-seven, she married the love of her life Pastor Marlon Lock. They have four beautiful daughters and a son. Kim has built a spiritual atmosphere in her home, where she balances the delicate tasks of nurturing and guiding her children. By the time her daughters were two years old, they could pray the Lord's Prayer, sing in the choir and praise dance. This dedicated mother resigned her position as Project Manager/Systems Analyst for National Life Insurance Company to raise her children.

Kim assists her husband in the business aspects of running Unity Gospel House of Prayer, Milwaukee, Wisconsin, which has several thousand members. In addition, she is a soloist in the choir and a member of the church's Praise Dance Team. Kimberly also manages UGHOP's website, Facebook and Twitter, which broadcast weekly messages of spiritual encouragement. She is also the mother of five children.

Women from all walks of life are drawn to her for spiritual guidance. Her character is calm and meek, while her style is simply "classy." She is a woman of few and selected words, reflecting her passionate devotion to the Lord and her heart's commitment to developing women spiritually. You're invited to join the author and other once silly, now virtuous women at www.WhoYouCallinSilly.com.

Acknowledgments

To my Lord and Savior Jesus Christ: without you, there is no me.

To my husband and my Pastor, Marlon: we began this journey of marriage not knowing that ANY of this would transpire. Let's continue to do what we have always done, which is follow the Lord wherever He leads us.

To my children, Toney, India, Asia, Sydney and Marlon Jr.: I love you dearly and the heavens (not the sky) are the limit for you.

To my mothers, Edna (birth mom) and Thelma (inherited through marriage): thanks for stepping in when I needed you. Although you had no idea what I was doing, you didn't question. Ma, you broke the stereotype of raising a child as a single parent, always denying you for me! I am thankful for our relationship and I am truly blessed to have a mother like you with your country self. You can take the lady from the country, but you can't take the country out the lady. Ha ha ha. You wondered and were "inquisitive" (we call it nosey) but you didn't ask any questions. Love you. Thelma (a.k.a. Pretty Jean Shankapoo), thanks for stepping in, just always being there when you could and accepting me as your daughter. One thing I love and admire about you all is that you never use the word "step" or "in laws" and you treated me as if I were your birth daughter. I sincerely appreciate that. I even appreciate the "DUH" moments you had when you would pretend like you didn't understand when we wanted you to watch the kids. Ha Ha Ha. If anyone knows, you all KNOW how Sydney can be, with herself. LOL.

To my "sisters," you know who you are: yes, you knew about the book on the DL. Not supposed to let your left hand know what your right hand is doing but shucks, I had too much emotion going on…birth of our first son and the thought of ME writing a book…I needed someone I could send excerpts to and you all were always there. What do we always say? "If the Lord is blessing my neighbor, He's in my neighborhood" so get ready to continue on this journey with me! I love you as if we all have the same mom and dad.

To Miss Naomi, a.k.a. Grandma: you know you're spicy, but you know we wouldn't change anything about you. Thank you for your wisdom and knowledge that you have shared with us, which you gathered in your sixty-one years of marriage to Paw, and for living a life well-pleasing unto the Lord. Now that he's gone on, you still have your travelling shoes on, so keep-a-going!

To Granny, a.k.a. Mother Moore: you were SUCH a huge part of my upbringing. At one point, folks thought I was your daughter because we travelled so much together and when you walked in church, I was right there with you. Thank you for teaching us respect and love and going to the farm picking string beans, strawberries and greens and then showing us how to can them (although we never did, LOL). I love you.

To all my aunts, uncles, cousins, nieces and nephews near and far I love you all regardless of the paths we've taken. Let's get together and have one big family reunion. It's long overdue. Get out your feelings and any issues you have with one another, get over them and become closer. Life is too short to hold on to stuff of no value.

To my middle school/college friends/co-workers Tiffany Dillon (a.k.a. Tiffie), Chrisetta (a.k.a. Chrissy) Jackson, Mackenzie (a.k.a. Mack) Blackmon, Bernadette (a.k.a. Bernie) Williams: thanks for being YOU and never changing. It's funny how when we all worked for the same company or when we'd have our girl pow-wow's, someone would have some big news of marriage, back to school, pregnancy, moving out of town, re-enlisting in the army, the list goes on; I'm sorry I waited to spill the beans until now on this one, but I have a strange feeling that you all will forgive me and I'll probably be getting calls and email from one or more of you! :0 Love you!

To Natosha Dooling: you and your family became an extension of our family when you joined our church while your husband played for the Milwaukee Bucks. It was during this time that your book was published and you spoke at our women's retreat on how your book came about. Unknowingly, I believe the Lord brought you all there for ME! He places people in our lives for a reason and the reason for me was to begin this journey of writing a book and to acquire another sister and a brother. Thanks for taking time out of your hectic schedule when I needed you most! We talked about our purpose of spreading this Word and that's what we are doing. As you wrap your arm around mine and we walk shoulder to shoulder, let's press on; you encourage me and I encourage you as we fulfill our destiny. Love you dearly!

To my dad, simply stated, I love you—always have and always will. I'm ready when you are and I am still your "Kimmie."

To Rhonda (RC): thanks, sis, for always being there when I need you!

TO THE GREATEST CHURCH FAMILY IN THE WORLD…. UNITY GOSPEL HOUSE OF PRAYER!!! You all are amazing. Not ever did my husband and I think we'd be Pastor and wife. My husband always thought he would be the assistant to his granddad and that was fine with him, but God was ready to call His servant home, Apostle Elbridge Lock, who worked diligently for the Kingdom. Thank you Unity for your love and support! Are you all ready? Get ready…as our motto is: "If you obey God, He will bless you realllll good!"

Notes

1. Bible, King James Version (KJV)
2. "Silly." Merriam-Webster.com. 2011. http://www.merriam-webster.com (14 Oct 2011).
3. "Laden." Merriam-Webster.com. 2011. http://www.merriam-webster.com (14 Oct 2011).
4. "Rib Cage." Wikipedia.org. 2011. http://www.en.wikipedia.org/wiki/Rib_cage (18 Oct 2011).
5. "Help." Merriam-Webster.com. 2011. http://www.merriam-webster.com (4 Nov 2011).
6. "Meet." Merriam-Webster.com. 2011. http://www.merriam-webster.com (4 Nov 2011).

www.ingramcontent.com/pod-product-compliance
Lightning Source LLC
Chambersburg PA
CBHW080411300426
44113CB00015B/2481